Praise for *In Search of the King*

I have had the pleasure of working with Thann Bennett for many years. I know his passion and his desire to serve the Lord. *In Search of the King* is an informative and inspirational read. It is a must read.

—Jay Sekulow
Chief Counsel of the American Center for Law and Justice
and *New York Times* best-selling author

I've run hard after many goals in my life—everything from the Olympics to the US Congress. Those pursuits pale in comparison to a true, lifelong discovery of the King. Thann's message in *In Search of the King* will breathe life into your pursuit of the King and will challenge you to make service in His court the highest priority of your life.

—Jim Ryun
Olympian, former world record holder,
and former Member of US Congress

You were created by someone bigger than you for a story larger than your own. *In Search of the King* will inspire you to discover a more intimate, more passionate, and more authentic relationship with the One who has been pursuing you since the beginning of time. Thann Bennett's very personal and engaging style will captivate your heart and imagination and send you on a relentless journey to learn the character of Jesus, walk in His ways, and join His mission. Enjoy the journey!

—Heather Zempel
Discipleship Pastor at National Community Church
and author of *Sacred Roads*, *Community Is Messy*,
and *Amazed and Confused*

In Search of the King is about the most important journey anyone can take. One day we will all meet the King, but a wealth of joy and abundant life is waiting for those of us who find the King in this life. *In Search of the King* will lead you on an epic journey in which you will find yourself face-to-face with the King, and when you come face-to-face with the King there is nothing that will give you more hope, joy, and satisfaction.

—Ryan Hall
Olympian and fastest US marathoner in history

Thann thoroughly exposes and explores the profound mystery of the entangled identity of God and man while challenging us to discover its mandates and rewards.

—John Ashcroft
Attorney General of the United States (2001–2005)

Thann Bennett has given us all a wonderful gift. *In Search of the King* is as uplifting as it is challenging. If there is one thing that eludes so many Christians, it is an appreciation of the kingship of Christ. It seems we either place Jesus so high on a throne that we cannot relate to Him, or, we diminish His majesty and mar His greatness so we can relate to Him. Thann shows a way to avoid both spiritual errors and find the wonderful relationship we can all have with the King of Glory!

—Rev. Rob Schenck, D.Min.
President, Faith and Action in the Nation's Capital

Practical and biblical! *In Search of the King* takes a very big issue for many—finding meaning—and makes it palatable. Give this book to anyone looking for purpose!

—Joshua Symonette
Campus Pastor at National Community Church and former NFL player

In an age that prefers rights over responsibilities, autonomy over accountability, and self-expression over self-surrender, the refrain, "O, how I love Your law!" has become increasingly rare—and we are reaping dire consequences spiritually, culturally, and socially. Wise souls, on the other hand, understand that the only life worth living is the one in which heart, soul, strength, and mind are aligned with the Creator's design for human flourishing. Thann Bennett's book, *In Search of the King*, provides such wise souls with an excellent road map. I highly recommend this book.

—Scott Sauls
Senior Pastor of Christ Presbyterian Church in Nashville, Tennessee,
and author of *Jesus Outside the Lines* and *Befriend*

In Search of the King is an insightful reminder that we already have a wise, just, and powerful King who knows our needs and recognizes our frailty. If we have forgotten that there is someone greater than ourselves, this is a wonderful spiritual jog for our memory.

—James Lankford
United States Senator, Oklahoma

In Search of the King will inspire and stimulate everyone from the greatest in academia to the occasional reader. Thann's writing weaves personal illustrations with biblical applications in a way that motivates readers to action. You will walk away from reading this book determined to discover greater intimacy with God while walking in an ever-deeper realization of your life's purpose!

—Victor Marx
Founder, All Things Possible Ministries

In Search of the King challenged me to take stock of my own walk with Jesus. Am I discovering new things about Him each day? Am I becoming less so that He can become more? Is my life yielded to His service so that His amazing work is being accomplished? Thann Bennett led me on a journey of realizing what I have longed for all along—that no matter where I am or what I am doing, I want to be found in the life altering presence of the King.

—Susanna Foth Aughtmon
Author of *Queen of the Universe: Encouragement for Moms and Their World Changing Work*

When we hear the word *king* it's easy to think in terms of earthly political power. And Thann Bennett would certainly be qualified to speak on that, given his many years cruising the marble halls of Capitol Hill in Washington D.C. But this wonderful book focuses on another kind of kingdom and a very different kind of King—Christ, the King of kings and Lord of lords. Immersed in Scripture and thoroughly practical, *In Search of the King* is a powerful reminder that amid a culture that too often emphasizes self-indulgence, Jesus calls us to a life of service and obedience perfectly exemplified by our high and holy King, Jesus Christ.

—Craig Parshall
Best-selling author of *The Occupied* and Special Counsel, ACLJ
—Janet Parshall
Nationally syndicated radio talk show host

IN SEARCH OF THE KING

OF THE

TURNING YOUR DESIRE *for* MEANING *into* *the* DISCOVERY *of* GOD

THANN BENNETT

WORTHY®
PUBLISHING

Published by Worthy Books, an imprint of Worthy Publishing Group, a division of Worthy Media, Inc., One Franklin Park, 6100 Tower Circle, Suite 210, Franklin, TN 37067.

WORTHY is a registered trademark of Worthy Media, Inc.

HELPING PEOPLE EXPERIENCE THE HEART OF GOD

eBook available wherever digital books are sold.

Library of Congress Cataloging-in-Publication Data

Names: Bennett, Thann, author.
Title: In search of the king : turning your desire for meaning into the
    discovery of God / by Thann Bennett.
Description: Franklin, TN : Worthy Publishing, 2017. | Includes
    bibliographical references.
Identifiers: LCCN 2016053318 | ISBN 9781617958588 (tradepaper)
Subjects: LCSH: Spirituality--Christianity. | Jesus Christ--Royal office.
Classification: LCC BV4501.3 .B4577 2017 | DDC 248.4--dc23
LC record available at https://lccn.loc.gov/2016053318

Published in association with Shannon Marven, DuPree/Miller & Associates, Dallas, TX.

For foreign and subsidiary rights, contact rights@worthypublishing.com.

ISBN: 978-1-61795-858-8
Cover Design: Bill Chiaravalle | Brand Navigation
Interior Design and Typesetting: Bart Dawson

Printed in the United States of America
17 18 19 20 21 LBM 5 4 3 2 1

You will seek me and find me
when you seek me with all your heart.
Jeremiah 29:13

May these pages channel the boundless Word of God,
making their reach limitless and timeless,
according to 2 Timothy 2:9.

To Brooke, my one and only, forever.

CONTENTS

FOREWORD

by Mark Batterson

·····━━━━━◆━━━━━·····

The book you are holding in your hands is a dream. In fact, it's a dream two times over.

This book, *In Search of the King*, started out as a dream that God planted in Thann's heart in February 2001. That dream lay dormant for nearly fifteen years. But as with all God-given dreams, God patiently nurtured it to fruition. I know this backstory because I have the privilege of being part of it. I have observed this dream, believed in this dream, and spoken into this dream for more than a decade now as Thann's pastor.

On April 19, 2015, I preached a sermon titled "The Art of the Start." It was part of a series titled One Little Yes. I asked a simple question at the outset of that series: "What do you need to start?" That question was coupled with a challenge:

"You cannot finish what you do not start." Of course, the first step is always the hardest.

The following morning, I received a number of e-mails from people who were at long last saying yes to the dreams God had given them, and Thann was one of them. I think it was Thann's way of going public with his dream and holding himself accountable. He made a commitment at the altar to quit delaying. In fact, he took the first step of faith by writing a thousand words. It was a victory for Thann and gratifying for me.

As an author, I knew better than most the challenges Thann would confront as he wrote, but after more than fourteen years, the dream God had placed in his heart had finally left the starting blocks.

As fate—or God's sense of humor—would have it, I left for sabbatical shortly after responding to Thann's e-mail. But I covered his efforts in prayer and was eager to check in with him when I returned. There would be no check-in necessary, however, as God's message to Thann had been waiting to spill out of him. By the time I returned from sabbatical, there was a fifty-thousand-word manuscript waiting in my in-box!

You will read more about this story from Thann's perspective later in these pages, but there is a reason I share it with you at the outset. It is because of the second way in which you are holding a dream—your dream. I believe that the God of the universe—the very King these pages will introduce you to—places His dreams in each of us on a regular basis. This book will not only pull that dream out of you, but it will spur you into channeling that dream into service of the King.

This book is going to challenge your walk with the Savior King. It is going to call you into a new discovery of Him, new ways to serve Him. You will be tempted to delay, but I plead with you to resist that temptation. You are holding this book—this dream—for a reason. The King wants to do a new thing in you and through you. He wants to reveal Himself to you in a way you have not experienced before. He longs to know you more intimately and to be more fully known by you.

As this book calls you into that discovery, do not put it off until a more convenient time. Make a commitment to truly discover the King, and then box yourself in to that commitment by telling someone you trust.

My spiritual father, Dick Foth, often reminds me of God's desire: "Tell them who I am, not what I do." That is what this book does. It proclaims the name and identity of the King. More specifically, it will inspire you to go on your own search for the King and to experience your own unique discovery of Him. You will find a new clarity about who the King is and a new understanding of how to actively walk with Him and daily dialogue with Him. You will be challenged to step into even bigger and better dreams because you will understand anew that you are invited to walk in the power of the King each and every day. Most importantly, these pages will leave you hungry for more of the King.

I caution you: The message of this book will challenge you to action. Yes, you will be inspired and encouraged, because you will better know what it means to discover the King. But do not mistake inspiration and encouragement for comfort, because you are about to be made uncomfortable. No matter where you are in your journey with the King, He is calling you to a new and deeper intimacy with Him. There is another layer of service to Him—one that involves even more of His power working through you. These pages will leave you unwilling to stay where you are.

So yes, you are holding a dream. I mean it both literally (this book) and figuratively (your life). I believe with all my heart that each and every person holding this book—that means you—has a God-sized dream planted deep inside. You may even be holding *on to* a dream rather than stepping with courage *into* that dream. That dream involves—and even requires—a deeper discovery of the King's character and His power. As you embark on this journey to tap into that power, I challenge you to do it with your own dream in mind.

What is your dream?

Have you invited the King to lead you into a discovery of it?

Have you committed yourself to it?

Are you content to continue holding on to that dream? Or are you ready to finally let it loose and chase after it?

I hope you will choose the chase, because it is that pursuit that will lead you into a discovery of the King. It is time to set off *in search of the King*.

INTRODUCTION
Where Is the King?

W here is the King?"

This is a question that nearly all of us ask at some point in life, but many of us never fully find the answer. It seems as if the King we are searching for is constantly moving just out of our reach. We think that if we could run a little harder or search a little better, we would find Him.

But I have news for you. We will never find the King as a result of a frantic search. We cannot find Him by trying harder, running faster, or arriving at our destination sooner. If we are to discover the King our hearts are longing for, it will happen not at the end of our life's journey but in the midst of it. Our discovery of the King is not about a destination; it is about a relationship.

An intimate knowledge of the King is something we discover piece by piece as we grapple with life while walking alongside Him. It is gritty. It is relational. And the key to this discovery lies in asking questions that create a daily dialogue with the King.

TURNING PURSUIT OF THE KING INTO DISCOVERY

In C. S. Lewis's book *The Horse and His Boy*,[1] Shasta is heir to the throne but does not realize it. He, along with his companion Aravis, has learned of a sinister plot to invade neighboring Archenland. Shasta and Aravis are desperate to reach Archenland to warn King Lune of the attack. They narrowly outrun the invading army and pass through the gates with precious little time to spare. But just as Shasta thinks his task is complete, he is informed that the king has gone on ahead and that he must carry the warning on foot.

Shasta is exhausted. He barely survived a dangerous dash to warn the king. He must have been thinking, *Why me? Surely someone else can take over the assignment from here.* Instead, Shasta asks, "Where is the king?" He does not insist on understanding why he has to complete the task, or even how he will find the strength. He simply asks to be pointed in the direction of the king. He asks which way he should run, and then he runs. In doing so, Shasta reveals the singular focus of his heart.

He wants to find the king.

Can you relate to Shasta in this story? Are you in a mad

dash to find the King? Or have you arrived at what you thought was your destination only to be told that the King is not there and that you must continue on foot? Are you exhausted and wondering if you will ever find Him, or questioning whether He exists at all?

When we are at a crossroads in life, we—like Shasta—need to ask the right questions in our search for the King. Once we are headed in the proper direction, we can turn our search for the King into a discovery of Him and a life of service to Him.

The key to finding the King is realizing that He is not waiting for us at some distant destination. We may think we are pursuing Him, but when we open our eyes, we will discover that He is already walking alongside us.

> I challenge you to simply ask, "Where is the King?" and to start off in that direction.

Are you at a crossroads in life where you must decide which direction to take? Are you asking, "Why me?" or, "How will I do this?" Instead, I challenge you to simply ask, "Where is the King?" and to start off in that direction. It may surprise you how quickly you will discover the King.

THE ONE WHO HAS LONG WAITED

After Shasta warns the king of the looming danger, he rides at the back of the king's army as they attempt to intercept the enemy. But Shasta becomes separated from the group and is desperately lost in a heavy fog. He is despondent to the point of tears until he is frightened by the startling realization that a giant creature is walking beside him. He cannot see the creature, but he can sense it and even feel its warm breath. Shasta considers making a run for it but quickly realizes that his horse is not up to the task. He then considers speaking to the creature but cannot muster the courage. So they proceed in silence.

As Shasta's terror continues to mount, he eventually whispers, "Who are you?"[2]

The answer Shasta receives is the same one we will hear when we finally decide to discover the King.

The creature responds, "One who has waited long for you to speak."[3]

Our King is walking alongside us—so close we can sense His presence and feel His mighty breath like a rushing wind.[4] He is standing guard over us. He is longing for relationship with us. Our King is desperate to know us and to be known by us. But He will never force Himself on us. He simply walks beside us and waits for us to speak.

Let us find the courage to speak and to embrace the

journey with Him that is freely available to us. Let us lay aside any fear that may be delaying that intimacy.

All we have to do is ask.

THE ONE WHO WALKS BESIDE US

One final tidbit from Shasta's encounter with the creature. The next several moments after Shasta speaks are spent engaging in conversation with the creature. The creature will not tell Shasta his identity but instead invites Shasta to tell of his sorrows. As Shasta does so, he is struck by his apparent misfortune at having encountered so many lions along his journey.

Here is the conversation that ensues between the creature and Shasta:

"There was only one lion," said the Voice.

"What on earth do you mean? I've just told you there were at least two lions the first night, and—"

"There was only one, but he was swift of foot."

"How do you know?"

"I was the lion."

And as Shasta gaped with open mouth and said nothing, the Voice continued. "I was the lion who forced you to join with Aravis. . . . I was the lion who drove the jackals from you as you slept. I was the lion who gave the Horses the new strength of fear for the last mile so that you should reach King Lune in time. And I was the lion you do not remember who pushed the boat in which you lay, a child near death, so that it came to shore where a man sat, wakeful at midnight, to receive you."[5]

Whether we realize it or not, the King is walking alongside us. He cares about our struggles, and He is intervening for us. He longs for our interaction and also for our acknowledgment and praise.

He is desperate for us to open our eyes in order to see Him.

He is desperate for us to open our ears in order to hear Him.

And He is desperate for us to open our mouths in order to converse with Him.

Make no mistake about it: our King wants a relationship with us. He will eagerly look upon us, speak to us, and fill our mouths that we may speak into the world around us. In fact, that is why He walks beside us, waiting for us to break the silence—*because He longs to reach the world through us.*

The time for our silence has come to an end. Let us learn to ask the proper questions as we encounter crossroads in our lives.

When we do not know where to turn, let us not ask where the various paths lead, but instead let us ask, *"Where is the King?"*

Let us be aware of the mighty power that walks alongside us and find the courage to ask, *"Who are you?"*

And finally, when we encounter the King in the faces and needs of those who surround us, let us ask, *"How can I serve?"*

If we ask these questions, we will discover so much more than a destination. We will discover the King

> Make no mistake about it: our King wants a relationship with us.

Himself. And better still, our search for *the* king will turn into a life of service to *the* King.

And every step of that journey will be taken alongside the very Lion of Judah who walks beside us (Revelation 5:5).

PART ONE

Search for the King

CHAPTER ONE

Who Is the King?

Who is he, this King of glory?

Psalm 24:10

T he President is here."

I was nineteen years old when I heard those words. The setting was a nondescript Washington, D.C., office building where I was volunteering my time to help George W. Bush transition into the presidency. It was a historic process, as the United States Supreme Court had just finalized the contested election in the case *Bush v. Gore*. While I was not particularly politically active at the time, I had several weeks to spare before the spring semester of school began, and I decided to spend them volunteering for the presidential transition. After all, it would provide a front-row seat to history.

There was only one problem: the presidential transition team was not looking for additional volunteers. They told me not to come because there was no room or need for me. So like any hardheaded teenager, I ignored their instructions; flew from Peoria, Illinois, to Washington, D.C.; and walked into the transition office with my résumé in hand. They again politely informed me that I was not needed. So I returned the following day. And the following day.

On the third day of my unannounced and uninvited arrivals, the transition staff finally relented and agreed to take me on. I spent the next several weeks doing every menial job I could find—from making coffee to running copies. There were a few more exciting and substantive jobs mixed in as well, but for the most part I did anything possible just to be a part of the team. I knew I was not an essential component of what was transpiring, and that was fine with me. I simply wanted to be present. My only real goal was to associate with something greater than myself.

After several weeks of long days and short nights, I was glad to have experienced the whirlwind of activity, but I was grateful to be approaching the end. I was exhausted.

Then the rushed whisper spread quickly through the building:

"The President is here."

With that short announcement, all fatigue vanished. Everyone from the most senior adviser to the lowliest volunteer (me) lined the perimeter of the largest room and waited with anticipation for our turn to greet the incoming President.

It was my first real brush with royalty. In the United States, we have presidents rather than kings, but in this context the distinction is insignificant. My nineteen-year-old self had been chasing an association with royalty, and I was about to experience it.

Each of us has a deep and abiding sense that we belong to someone or something greater. An instinctual understanding that we were created for something beyond ourselves. A longing to associate with royalty.

To put it plainly, at some point, each of us comes to a place in life where we feel the need for a king.

THE KINGS IN OUR CULTURE

Our own culture—like every one that has come before us and all that will come after—offers seemingly endless options to satisfy our longing for a king. We are surrounded by temptations to pursue power, fame, or other accolades. We are inundated with the allure of the celebrity, the impressive feats of the athlete, and the charisma of the spiritual or political leader. Each of these appeals to us in a different way, but each has the potential to become the object of our pursuit of a king.

While not everything about these pursuits is inherently wrong, none will satisfy our deepest longing. None will quench our thirst for a king. None will reveal the true character and identity of the King we seek.

> I simply wanted to be present. My only real goal was to associate with something greater than myself.

Nothing short of the one, true King of the universe can satisfy our abiding and divinely created desire for the King.

THE FUTILITY OF HUMAN KINGS

Our longing for a king has been visible in every culture and time. We know of countless examples where a people or a nation rushed to embrace a gregarious leader and place their trust and belief in him or her. In many cases, the result has been catastrophic. Consider the rise of Adolf Hitler in Nazi Germany. Hitler began as an adored politician but presided over the slaughter of approximately six million Jews and approximately five million others he deemed inferior. This phenomenon is in no way isolated to the past. As I write, political leaders in Syria are using chemical weapons on their own citizens, government officials in Sudan are at the center of an ongoing genocide within its borders, and the North Korean dictator has a habit of executing those who disagree with him—even if they are members of his family.

> We were made to commune with, worship, and serve the King.

History is replete with leaders who had an insatiable appetite for dominion and control. Because these leaders pursued selfish, earthly ambitions, the people suffered. In each of these cases, the people's misplaced effort to crown a physical king backfired on them.

In some cases, the rise of a dynamic leader appeared to succeed for a while, as that leader presided over a time of plenty. But when viewed through the lens of the eternal impact on individual souls, even this success is very fleeting. Our hearts were created for intimacy with the King. We were made to commune with, worship, and serve the King (Ephesians 1:12).

No matter how good a nation's leader may be, a human king simply cannot fulfill our longing for the King.

In 1 Samuel 8, the Israelites demanded a king to rule over them. Samuel warned the people that crowning a physical king would not only fail to address their needs but also would complicate their lives significantly. He warned that a king would take the best of their sons and daughters, as well as their fields and livestock.

Still the people insisted, "Give us a king to lead us" (v. 6).

So God granted the people their wish and appointed a king to rule over them. The result was a significant deterioration of the Israelites' relationship with the one, true King. The people missed the fact that crowning a human king would serve only to separate them from their real King.

When we try to force the crowning of a physical king in our lives, we do not address our need for the one and only King who is worthy to sit on the throne of our lives. In fact, it complicates our search for that King.

WHO IS THE KING?

Once we become aware of our deep longing and need for the King, the natural question is, "Who is the King?"

Who are we really searching for?

In Psalms, David frames the question like this: "Who is this King of glory?" (24:8). His question is both an acknowledgment of a desire for the one, true King and a query about the identity of that King. David is essentially asking, "I know this King is awesome and powerful, but just who, exactly, is He?"

This King should satisfy our desire to associate with something (or someone) greater than ourselves. His presence should comfort us and convey an abiding sense of belonging and security. This King, if He is to satisfy the innate longing in our souls, must be someone worthy of devoting our lives to, and He must be willing to accept us into His mission. He must deserve our praise yet desire our companionship.

This King must transcend this world yet be present in it with us.

There is only one King who can truly satisfy this longing in our souls. His identity is proclaimed by David as a response to his own question: "The LORD Almighty—he is the King of glory" (v. 10).

This conclusion might seem obvious to you. After all, Christians know plenty about the physical identity and character of our King. We even know His name—it is Jesus. In John 18, as Pilate was questioning Jesus, Pilate focused on the idea that Jesus was a king. In verse 37, Pilate asked Jesus, "So You are a king?" Jesus replied, "You say correctly that I am a king" (NASB). So if we are to believe Jesus, we know that He should be our King.

So why are so many of us still longing for a king? If we know intellectually that Jesus is the King, and we profess to know Him, they why does the longing persist?

In my own experience, this longing lingers when we are content with only a head knowledge of Jesus as the King but never truly discover what it means to walk daily with Him through service in His court. We think we know the King because we know His name, can recount facts about His life, and are familiar with many of His words. But our deep longing persists because we have yet to experience what it means for the King to be ruler of our lives in every way.

In John 6, after Jesus had performed the miracle of feeding the five thousand, the people were awed by Jesus's miracle yet deaf to His message. So they tried to force Jesus to be king—but in a physical, temporal sense rather than as the One who would sit on the eternal throne of their lives. The people accurately identified Jesus as the true King, but they failed to understand what His rule in their lives should look like. As a result, "Jesus, knowing that they intended to come and make him king by force, withdrew again to a mountain by himself" (John 6:15).

> There is only one King who can truly satisfy this longing in our souls.

THE KING OF KINGS

I invite you on a journey as we learn together how to search for, discover, and serve the King of kings, Jesus Christ. Our focus will not be on misplaced pursuits of an earthly king but on how we can and will find the one, true King. We will learn how to see the King in our everyday encounters. We will experience the life-changing discovery that our search for the King is not conducted in His absence but rather right alongside Him. We will learn how to recognize His face and how to enlist in His service.

Many of us have an academic understanding of the identity of the King, the character He possesses, and even the role He is supposed to fill in our lives. Yet a head knowledge of the identity of the King does nothing to satisfy our intense desire for Him.

> Our intimacy with the King goes far beyond simply understanding the identity of the King.

Our search for the King is aimed at something more. Our goal is not just understanding who the King is but also associating our name with His, intertwining our identity with His, and subjecting our goals and desires to those that He has for us. Our intimacy with the King goes far beyond simply understanding the identity of the King.

His name is Jesus, but who is He really? What is His character? What is His personality? What is His leadership style? And why do so many other things seem to crowd out our pursuit of Him? Why are we drawn to service of other "kings" in our lives?

I want to pose a pivotal question and then challenge each of us to linger on it for a moment, because an honest contemplation will fundamentally change the way you pursue the King. In fact, it will transform your search for the King into your discovery of the King.

The question is this: If we have a desire for the King, and if we know who that King is, then why are we still searching for Him instead of serving Him?

It is this shift between knowing the identity of the King and actually enlisting in His service that we will pursue in these pages. In this book we will explore what it means to submit to the kingship of Jesus and the fulfillment that comes from serving in His court.

THE KING'S FACE

Too often we have a disconnect between our mental understanding of the King and our practical recognition of Him. In other words, we are looking for the King when in reality He is all around us and we are failing to recognize Him. We are missing evidence of the King's work in our daily lives, and more importantly, we are failing to recognize the King's presence. Opportunities for service to the King are all around us, but we look right past them.

The simple truth is that we do not know the King's face—at least not as we should. So many times, our intentions are sound. We want to serve the King, and we are searching for ways to serve Him. But we have no idea what He looks like.

Think of someone you love deeply—maybe your spouse, parent, or child. When you think of that person, what image comes to mind? Their face, correct? When we love someone, we memorize their facial features and can recall them at a moment's notice—even long after they are gone. The face—and especially the eyes—is often called a window into the soul. So as we seek to know the character of our King, it is crucial that we learn to identify His face.

> We are told what the King's face looks like if we will just take the time to look.

As the old hymn urges us, "Turn your eyes upon Jesus / Look full in His wonderful face."[1] That type of intimacy requires a singular focus—an absolute dedication to knowing Him.

Fortunately, we are told what the King's face looks like if we will just take the time to look.

Consider this:

When the Son of Man comes in his glory, and all the angels with him, he will sit on his glorious throne. All the nations will be gathered before him, and he will separate the people one from another as a shepherd separates the sheep from the goats. He will put the sheep on his right and the goats on his left.

Then the King will say to those on his right, "Come, you who are blessed by my Father; take your inheritance, the kingdom prepared for you since the creation of the world. For I was hungry and you gave me something to eat, I was thirsty and you gave me something to drink, I was a stranger and you invited me in, I needed clothes and you clothed me, I was sick and you looked after me, I was in prison and you came to visit me."

Then the righteous will answer him, "Lord, when did we see you hungry and feed you, or thirsty and give you something to drink? When did we see you a stranger and invite you in, or needing clothes and clothe you? When did we see you sick or in prison and go to visit you?"

The King will reply, "Truly I tell you, whatever you did for one of the least of these brothers and sisters of mine, you did for me." (Matthew 25:31–40)

The King, on the day He comes in glory and assumes His eternal throne, will say, "Whatever you did for one of the least of these . . . you did for me." The rest of Matthew 25 deals with those who were divided on the left (the goats), and their verdict stands in stark contrast to the sheep, who were on the right: "Whatever you did not do for one of the least of these, you did not do for me" (v. 45).

When we stand before our King, our service (or lack thereof) to those around us will count as service (or lack thereof) to the King. When we encounter those around us, we must understand that each person reflects the image of our King. We must understand that service to those around us is service to our King.

> When we encounter those around us, we must understand that each person reflects the image of our King.

We are looking to prepare a feast for the King when the beggar on our street is hungry. *The beggar is the King.*

We are trying to place a royal robe on the King while many around us are cold and naked. *The cold and naked one among us is the King.*

We say we possess spiritual freedom for anyone who will accept it, yet countless among us remain spiritually bound. *The captive is the King.*

We are searching the ends of the earth for the King when our neighbor does not know Him. *Our neighbor is the King.*

We lament to a friend in need that we wish we knew how the King would have us help him. *That friend is the King.*

We talk with coworkers or church members about how to serve the King. *Those coworkers and church members are the King.*

We walk past stranger after stranger, looking for the face of the King. *The face of each of those strangers is the face of the King.*

The point is this: the King is everywhere we look. He is in our friendships, our workplaces, and the places of need that surround us. Opportunities to serve in His court are abundant. But it is impossible to serve the King until we can recognize His face.

Unlike the King's unchanging character, His face constantly takes on new identities in our lives. The face of Jesus is represented through new people, new needs, and new situations. While we should rejoice in what the King has done in days past, we cannot rest on yesterday's experience with Him as the way to recognize and embrace today's experience with Him. The King is the same yesterday, today, and forever (Hebrews 13:8), but it is easy to walk right past Him because we do not recognize His presence in our everyday encounters.

Do not walk past the King. Recognize the royalty that exists in the faces you encounter every day. Each of those faces is not just important to the King; each of those faces is a reflection of the King.

KING RODNEY

I have worked in the same office building for nearly ten years. I have walked the same street every day and have seen many of the same faces day after day. One of those faces belongs to a man named Rodney. Rodney walks with crutches because he has only one leg. He does not have a home or a family. He carries the few possessions he owns in a plastic bag he can manage with his crutches. You might think I know all of this because I have seen Rodney every day for almost ten years and have taken the time to get to know him.

But you would be wrong.

For nearly ten years, I had been only vaguely aware of Rodney's existence. I had seen him out of the corner of my eye but made no effort to truly notice him or the needs he may have had. I had been so focused on my tasks that I routinely walked past Rodney without so much as a sideways glance. I am ashamed to tell you: were it left to my own accord, I still would not know Rodney's name.

I know Rodney's name because of Ben. Ben is a coworker who joined our office recently. Ben shares my affinity for jalapeño burritos, so he has become a regular partner in my once-a-week (at least) walk for a burrito from my favorite nearby lunch place. One day as we walked, Ben was suddenly not with me. I realized he had stopped walking and talking in midsentence because he had spotted a friend. It was Rodney. I had once again walked past Rodney without even noticing him, but Ben had stopped and greeted him by name. Ben had seen Rodney for the first time just a few weeks earlier, yet he already knew his name. Meanwhile, I had been walking past Rodney for years.

As Ben and Rodney finished their brief conversation and Rodney starting working his crutches to move away from us, I noticed something. Rodney was wearing Ben's flannel shirt. He was wearing Ben's hiking boots. And he was carrying Ben's coat. I knew they were Ben's because I had seen them folded and stacked neatly in his office a few days earlier.

The image of Rodney walking away in Ben's clothes humbled me nearly to the point of tears. I suddenly realized that I had been walking right past the King for nearly ten years. The King had a name: Rodney. King Rodney had a very real and simple need: he was cold and without proper clothes and shoes. But I had paid no mind. And now King Rodney was walking away in Ben's clothes.

You see, Ben had sight where I had been blind. Ben recognized the King's face and learned his name. Ben saw King Rodney's simple need and met it. Ben could not change everything about King Rodney's reality, but he could ensure that King Rodney was warmer. So he did.

> I suddenly realized that I had been walking right past the King for nearly ten years.

As King Rodney walked away in Ben's clothes, I realized I had missed another encounter with the King. The question became personal in that moment: "Lord, when did *I* see You hungry and feed You, or thirsty and give You something to drink? When did *I* see You a stranger and invite

You in, or needing clothes and clothe You? When did *I* see You sick or in prison and go to visit You?"

The answer was the image of King Rodney walking away in Ben's clothes. I had been meditating on how to know the King, and I was pursuing Him the best way I knew how. But to truly discover the King, and to truly see His face, I had to finally notice King Rodney.

CHAPTER TWO
The King's Credentials

*The angel said to her, "Do not be afraid, Mary;
you have found favor with God. You will conceive
and give birth to a son, and you are to call him Jesus.
He will be great and will be called
the Son of the Most High. The Lord God
will give him the throne of his father David,
and he will reign over Jacob's descendants forever;
his kingdom will never end."*

Luke 1:30–33

I remember my first job interview as if it were yesterday. I was fifteen years old and had applied to work the grill at the local A&W root beer stand. I prepared as though it were my dream job. My résumé was polished and triple-checked, and I made sure to arrive early. The owner had told me the interview would be short because she only had a few minutes to spare before opening the store. "Short" turned out to be an understatement, as the entire interview consisted of one two-part question: "When can you start, and which days can you work?" I had fretted over my résumé for nothing—it was never even read. I should have known better, because our family had known the owner's family for years. She did not need to see my résumé or ask me any questions. She already knew my credentials and my character, and she had based her decision on that knowledge.

As we continue our search for the King, it is imperative that we not only learn to see the King's face but also know His credentials and acquire His character. To accomplish this, we need to know not just what the King looks like but also who He is. We will start with His credentials. The Bible reveals

Jesus as our one, true King—by His heritage, His birth, His death, and most powerfully, His resurrection.

JESUS IS KING BY HERITAGE

John 1 is one of my favorite chapters in the Bible for many reasons, not the least of which is that it is where my namesake, Nathanael, makes a brief appearance. Only a few of Nathanael's words are recorded, most of which are tinged with doubt and skepticism. For example, Nathanael doubted that Jesus was the Messiah because He came from Nazareth—a place Nathanael considered to be unworthy. I have come to realize I am prone to the same type of doubt as my biblical namesake and must take great care to avoid passing judgment on people because of where they come from or what they have experienced. However, it is Nathanael's declaration of Jesus's kingship I want to focus on here.

> If we are convinced enough to say, "You are the Son of God," then we must also say, "You are King over my life."

To set the scene, Jesus was in the process of calling His disciples. Philip was trying to persuade Nathanael that Jesus was the Messiah. Nathanael was unconvinced until Jesus demonstrated His intimate knowledge of Nathanael. As a result, Nathanael was convinced of Jesus's deity and His power. His response, linking Jesus's association with the Father and His kingship, is significant:

Nathanael declared, "Rabbi, you are the Son of God;
you are the king of Israel." (John 1:49)

When Nathanael saw Jesus invoke divine authority, he realized that Jesus was the Son of God. But why did Nathanael then call Him the "king of Israel"? The answer is that when Nathanael submitted to the Son of God, he automatically recognized Him as King. Nathanael understood that the Son of God would be King over Israel and King over his life. Therefore, when Nathanael met Jesus and the first part of that puzzle fell into place, he automatically linked the "Son of God" with the "king of Israel."

Jesus is King because He is the Son of the Father.

Jesus is King because He has been sent by the Father.

Jesus is King because of His heritage.

When we are convinced of Jesus's heritage—the fact that He is indeed the Son of God—then His kingship over our lives should be automatic. If we are convinced enough to say, "You are the Son of God," then we must also say, "You are King over my life." I confess that this is many times an unnatural response for me. But if I truly believe Jesus is the Son of God, how can I possibly justify giving Him anything less than everything?

The first part of this equation (convincing us of the deity of Jesus) is God's responsibility. But the response is up to us.

Jesus is King by heritage. It is our job to accept that truth and proclaim it.

JESUS IS KING BY BIRTH

I want to take a fresh look at the miraculous birth of divine royalty. Because the birth of Jesus is such a familiar story, we tend to tune out and miss the subtleties. I challenge you to imagine yourself in the place and time where Jesus was born, and consider not only the practical miracle (*Jesus was conceived by the Holy Spirit within a virgin*) but also the scandal (*the conception of Jesus spelled disaster or even possible death for Jesus's earthly mother*) and especially the magnificent royal fanfare (*visits from wise men and proclamations from heaven*) that accompanied the arrival of Jesus.

This is the story of the arrival of a long-awaited King. It is a miracle that commands our attention. More specifically, it is the announcement of an arrival that commands our attention:

> The angel said to her, "Do not be afraid, Mary; you have found favor with God. You will conceive and give birth to a son." (Luke 1:30–31)

The news that a baby is on the way should be the best news a parent ever receives. It should carry with it hopes and dreams for new life and the joy of family. But if the birth of our King were a dramatic production, this prelude would be labeled a tragedy. The angel delivered news to Mary that was not only physically impossible but decidedly frightening. If Mary, an unwed girl, was pregnant, she would be an outcast. Her husband-to-be would almost certainly abandon her, her community would view her as unclean, and in all likelihood her child would be rejected by the world.

It was an indescribably difficult situation for Mary (and for Joseph as well). This seems like a lousy way to bring the King into the world. A king is supposed to arrive with fanfare and rejoicing. He is supposed to be the object of overwhelming affection, not the subject of scorn and rejection. Yet the angel revealed that this very attribute of Jesus's arrival communicated the authority of His kingship.

You are to call him Jesus. He will be great and will be called the Son of the Most High. (vv. 31–32)

Allow me the liberty of paraphrasing the angel's words: "Mary, this Child within you, who seems as if He represents the death of all your hopes and dreams—He already has a name. It is Jesus, and it is your job to tell the world His name. He already has an identity. That identity is found in His Father and carries with it a royal title."

I believe—and Scripture confirms[1]—that Jesus's entry into the world was simple and humble in order to communicate this truth: the great worth of Jesus was not rooted in stature or earthly merit, but rather in the name He was bestowed and the royal lineage into which He was born.

He was conceived in what appeared to be scandal. But His mother called Him Jesus. And the heavens called Him the Son of the Most High.

> The Lord God will give him the throne of his father David, and he will reign over Jacob's descendants forever; his kingdom will never end. (vv. 32–33)

Not only was this Child given a name and an association that foretold His greatness, but He was also given a throne. It is worth noting that in one short announcement, the angel communicated that Jesus would reign over both a heavenly kingdom and an earthly kingdom.

Jesus was given a name and an identity that made Him great. That name makes Him heir to a throne. That throne makes Him King.

Jesus is King by birth.

Now, with that glorious declaration of royalty, I want to return to the opening line delivered by the angel to Mary:

> The angel said to her, "Do not be afraid, Mary; you have found favor with God." (v. 30)

Mary was afraid for good reason. From her perspective, this was anything but good news. It was certainly not risk-free news! Mary's fear was so visible that the angel opened with an instruction to lay aside her fear and an assurance that she had found favor with God.

This is another takeaway from the preamble that we should not miss: if we desire to be a part of the King's story, then we often have to set aside our fear.

Notice that the angel acknowledges Mary's fear. But she is instructed, "Do not be afraid."

All too often I have misapplied this principle in my life. I have sought opportunities and tasks that are free from fear. I have selected things to do based on what frightens me the least. This approach will cause us to miss out on significant portions of the King's story that we are being called into. Like Mary, we are called to take the name of the King into places where it is not yet known. In our world, this assignment carries with it a practical cause for fear. There is reason to fear our association with the King if we focus on the circumstances. But we are instructed to focus on the name of the King. We

> The great worth of Jesus was not rooted in stature or earthly merit, but rather in the name He was bestowed and the royal lineage into which He was born.

are commanded to make His name known. And we are assured by a voice that says, "Do not be afraid."

Jesus is King by virtue of His birth. And we are called to fearlessly proclaim His name.

JESUS IS KING BY DEATH

Jesus's crucifixion is one of history's most well-known stories and is probably the event that is most commonly associated with His kingship. It is easy to overlook the fact that the crucifixion was not simply an act of obedience by Jesus in order to fulfill prophecies and atone for the sins of the world (though it was certainly that).[2] Jesus's death was also a confirmation of His kingship. In fact, the kingship of Jesus was central to the case brought against Him and was the ultimate reason He was put to death.

> Jesus's death on the cross affirmed His claim as the Eternal King.

The four Gospels each give an account of the events leading up to Jesus's death. While each reflects a unique perspective on what transpired, together these New Testament accounts record this important point: Jesus's death on the cross affirmed His claim as the Eternal King.

I am especially struck by the exchange between Pontius Pilate, Jesus, and the people who were demanding Jesus's crucifixion in John 18:28–19:16.

Pilate was the Roman governor, and the people brought

Jesus to him after they had failed to earn a conviction of Jesus from Caiaphas, the high priest. This failure was significant, because Caiaphas was sympathetic to the people's desire to put Jesus to death and agreed that, "It would be good if one man died for the people" (John 18:14). But Caiaphas was unable to find evidence to support a guilty verdict. So the people brought Jesus to Pilate.

When Jesus was handed over to Pilate, the first significant exchange was between Pilate and the people:

> Pilate came out to them and asked, "What charges are you bringing against this man?"
>
> "If he were not a criminal," they replied, "we would not have handed him over to you."
>
> Pilate said, "Take him yourselves and judge him by your own law."
>
> "But we have no right to execute anyone," they objected. (vv. 29–31)

Pilate was looking for evidence, but the people had none—or at least they had none that gave them a right to execute Jesus, which is what they wanted. They needed Pilate to find a charge that would warrant execution.

The next significant exchange was between Pilate and Jesus, and it centered on the question of whether Jesus was a king:

Pilate then went back inside the palace, summoned Jesus and asked him, "Are you the king of the Jews?"

"Is that your own idea," Jesus asked, "or did others talk to you about me?"

"Am I a Jew?" Pilate replied. "Your own people and chief priests handed you over to me. What is it you have done?"

Jesus said, "My kingdom is not of this world. If it were, my servants would fight to prevent my arrest by the Jewish leaders. But now my kingdom is from another place."

"You are a king, then!" said Pilate.

Jesus answered, "You say that I am a king. In fact, the reason I was born and came into the world is to testify to the truth. Everyone on the side of truth listens to me." (vv. 33–37)

Pilate wanted to appease the people, so he considered the possibility that Jesus's claim to be a king was a challenge to Caesar's authority. Jesus did not refute the idea that He was a king, but He was clear that His kingdom was not of this world and thus was not a challenge to Caesar.

Pilate was caught in the middle. He wanted to please the people, but he could not find cause to sentence Jesus to death. So he tried to trap Jesus one final time by declaring, "You are a king, then!" (v. 37).

Jesus answered that He "came into the world . . . to testify to the truth" (v. 37). He admitted His own kingship, but without any challenge attached. His response left Pilate more confused than ever.

As a result, Pilate punished Jesus by having Him flogged. Then, as an act of ridicule toward Jesus's claim of kingship, Jesus was dressed in a purple robe, adorned with a crown of thorns, and abused both verbally and physically by Pilate's guards. But when Pilate returned Jesus to the people in this humiliating fashion, he did so with these words: "Look, I am bringing him out to you to let you know that I find no basis for a charge against him" (John 19:4).

> Jesus understood that His death was tied to His kingship.

The people responded with relentless demands to crucify Jesus, to which Pilate finally responded, "You take him and crucify him. As for me, I find no basis for a charge against him" (v. 6).

Even this did not satisfy the people, who were desperate to share the responsibility for crucifying Jesus. As their exchange continued, Pilate demanded of Jesus, "Do you refuse to speak to me? Don't you realize I have power either to free you or to crucify you?" (v. 10).

Jesus responded by pointing to His eternal kingdom: "You would have no power over me if it were not given to you from above" (v. 11).

Jesus understood that His death was tied to His kingship. He embraced the reality that this moment of darkness played a significant role in ushering in His eternal kingdom. He acknowledged that Pilate had the authority to order His death but clarified that the Giver of that authority rules over a much greater kingdom—a kingdom over which Jesus Himself reigns.

Finally, Pilate handed Jesus over to the people to be crucified (v. 16). And he fastened a sign to His cross that read, "JESUS OF NAZARETH—THE KING OF THE JEWS" (v. 19).

Jesus is King by death.

Upon encountering that death, Jesus declared, "It is finished" (v. 30). By completing His act of laying down His life for us, His kingship was further realized.

But the story of Jesus was not finished, and neither was the King's reign. As important as it is to know that Jesus is King by His heritage, birth, and death, all of those are simply a prelude to the crescendo that is knowing Him as the Eternal King who has defeated death and is reigning now and forever.

In my opinion, one of the most compelling prophecies about this next stage of kingdom pursuit came from the King Himself as He hung on the cross. As the physical life of Jesus was seeping out of Him, He reminded us that His death was anything but the end. Jesus's death would, instead, usher in

His eternal kingdom. As we will see, the beauty of His promise was enhanced by the fact that it was issued to someone who did not deserve it. It contains an assurance for each of us that Jesus's eternal kingdom will also be our eternal kingdom if we will simply place ourselves in association with Him.

JESUS IS REIGNING KING
BY RESURRECTION

Of all of Jesus's royal characteristics, this is the one that seals the deal and provides us a share of eternity: Jesus is King by resurrection.

Here is what Jesus declared about His eternal kingdom:

One of the criminals who hung there hurled insults at him: "Aren't you the Messiah? Save yourself and us!"

But the other criminal rebuked him. "Don't you fear God," he said, "since you are under the same sentence? We are punished justly, for we are getting what our deeds deserve. But this man has done nothing wrong."

Then he said, "Jesus, remember me when you come into your kingdom."

Jesus answered him, "Truly I tell you, today you will be with me in paradise." (Luke 23:39–43)

Acceptance into the eternal kingdom happens through a simple act of belief. As the life of the repentant criminal ebbed out of him, his words conveyed two concepts: he acknowledged his wrongdoing and the innocence of the King, and he asked the King for permission to associate with Him.

Let us not overcomplicate the gift of eternal life. To be sure, a life of service to the King should cause us to desire a deeper knowledge of the King. But let us not be so pious as to project upon others more requirements for receiving the saving grace of the King than the King Himself did!

> Because of His resurrection and victory over death, the Eternal King is now reigning and will reign forever and ever.

Romans 10:9 says, "If you declare with your mouth, 'Jesus is Lord,' and believe in your heart that God raised him from the dead, you will be saved." In his dying moments, the criminal did exactly that. He did not know the sinner's prayer or complex theology. But he knew he was a sinner, and he recognized his need for the Eternal King hanging next to him. That criminal would not have an opportunity for lengthy service in the King's court here on earth, but he was welcomed with open arms into the eternal kingdom by the King Himself.

The King put it this way: "Truly I tell you, today you will be with me in paradise" (Luke 23:43).

The King knew that His kingdom awaited Him. But the timing of that kingdom is significant. The criminal seemed uncertain about when that reign would begin and asked only to be remembered when the time came. The King responded with the promise that they would be together in paradise *that same day*.

Because of His resurrection and victory over death, the Eternal King is now reigning and will reign forever and ever. As we strive to know His face and serve in His court on this side of eternity, let us follow the example of the King and pave a simple path for people to find Him. Let us encourage those who know Him to grow in a deeper knowledge of Him, but let us simply call those who are lost into an immediate association with the King and an assurance of paradise.

Jesus is King by resurrection. He is reigning forever and ever. And each of us has a place with Him in paradise if we will simply believe.

CHAPTER THREE
The Eternal King

The kingdom of the world has become
the kingdom of our Lord and of his Messiah,
and he will reign for ever and ever.

Revelation 11:15

I love old T-shirts. If left to my own devices, I would wear an old T-shirt every day. There is something about the combination of comfort from repeated wear and the nostalgia of where the shirt came from that just feels right to me. As a result, I own more T-shirts than I should. *Many more!* My wife, Brooke, is baffled by my inability to let go of what is essentially a faded, stained remnant of the past. She is, of course, correct that I should not be clinging to something that has outlived its worth. Yet I have a very hard time letting go. In fact, it is precisely that tie to the past that gives me pause.

When I wear an old T-shirt, others see simply an old T-shirt. But I remember what that T-shirt signifies. I remember the teammates who wore identical shirts as we competed together or the good memories of the road race I ran in that T-shirt. I know it is trite and I recognize the juvenile folly of it even as I write, but the simple fact is that T-shirts are for me a tangible reminder of good times in the past, and I am wired to cling to those times.

In reality, we are all wired to cling to old garments.

While you likely do not share my bizarre attachment to worn-out T-shirts, there is a very good likelihood you share my inclination to remain adorned in the spiritual clothing of the past. Hebrews 12:1 calls on us to "throw off everything that hinders" us, but we are inexplicably attached to temporal things that should be left behind.

The book of Revelation repeatedly reminds us that there is a white garment or a white robe that awaits each of us.[1] These are eternal garments, but they also illustrate what our perspective should be today. As we begin our search for the Eternal King, our focus should not be on things of the past, and not even on things present, but rather on things yet to come—the things of Jesus's eternal kingdom that will not pass away.

A NEW THING

So how do we choose to focus on our eternal clothing—our white robe of the Eternal King's court? It requires both a familiarity with the King and the boldness to truly step into a new thing.

Through the prophet Isaiah, God declared:

See, I am doing a new thing!
    Now it springs up; do you not perceive it?
I am making a way in the wilderness
    and streams in the wasteland. (Isaiah 43:19)

Notice that God's call to step into a new thing presents a two-part challenge for us.

Look Toward the Future

First, the new thing into which we are called is already happening. The King is already on the move and is already engaged in the new thing. He is asking whether we have noticed. Are we looking toward the future, or are our eyes focused on that which lies behind us?

The verses immediately preceding Isaiah 43:19 point to the mighty acts the King has already accomplished: "This is what the LORD says—he who made a way through the sea, a path through the mighty waters, who drew out the chariots and horses, the army and reinforcements together, and they lay there, never to rise again, extinguished, snuffed out like a wick" (vv. 16–17).

In this passage, the King had just brought His people through the Red Sea on dry land and wiped out the army that had been pursuing them. His display of power was worthy of looking back on. Surely it was an act that should be dwelled on. Or was it?

The next verse rejects the notion of dwelling on the past: "Forget the former things; do not dwell on the past" (v. 18).

Why would the King insist that we not dwell on what He has already accomplished for us? Why would He not revel in the praise and adoration that flow when we recall His great power? The answer lies in the fact that the Eternal King is doing a new thing. The King has already moved on to a new thing, and He wants us to live a dynamic life of experiencing His mighty power in the moment it happens. The King is doing a new thing to build His eternal kingdom, and His question to us is, "Do you not perceive it?"

Have we noticed what the King is now doing? It is humbling to think about how many times I may have missed an opportunity to experience the King's mighty power or grow in a deeper knowledge of His face because I was too focused on that which He has just brought me through. Ask yourself, "Am I focused on the King's face in such a way that I will perceive the new thing He is calling me to?"

Be Courageous

Second, the new thing into which we are called requires courage. Are we bold enough to step into a new thing? Remember Isaiah 43:19: "See, I am doing a new thing! Now it springs up; do you not perceive it? I am making a way in the wilderness and streams in the wasteland."

For those who belong to the King, an eternity of rest awaits us (Isaiah 57:2). But the King calls us through the wilderness and wastelands on this side of eternity. He assures us that He has made a way through these challenges on our behalf, but that way still leads us in a direction that requires us to depend on Him. He longs for an intimacy with us that comes only from walking through things that turn us back to Him. Those things may be challenges or struggles, or they may simply be things that feel beyond our capacity or comfort level.

In many ways, this book is part of my effort to learn this principle. It was February 2001 when I first knew God was asking me to write for Him. I found countless excuses and ways to tell God that He would have to wait until I was ready.

"God, I am not a pastor. I work in public policy."

"I am just beginning my career."

"I just do not have that kind of time."

I had a tremendous number of excuses, and all of them started with "I." They were all focused on my plan and my view of what lay ahead. I cringe to look back and admit that I walked in those excuses (and plenty more) for nearly fifteen years. The call to write was always simmering in the back of my mind, and it was reaffirmed numerous times by people close to me. Yet I continued to resist.

> "Am I focused on the King's face in such a way that I will perceive the new thing that He is calling me to?"

It was not until April 19, 2015, that I finally relented. God used the faithful voice of my pastor, Mark Batterson, to finally break through and cause me to choose obedience. On that Sunday morning as I knelt at the altar, it finally ceased to be about excuses. It finally ceased to be about me. It even finally ceased to be about the physical act of writing.

Instead, it was finally about obedience. For nearly fifteen years, the King had been asking me to write. I had chosen to condition my obedience on my own evaluation of the instruction. On that April morning, I finally understood that the new thing I was being called to had less to do with my own goals or station in life, and far more to do with stepping out in obedience into the new thing my King was doing. I grieved that I had resisted for so long, and I committed to begin immediately.

When we perceive the new thing the King is doing, will we be bold enough to follow? When that new thing you are called to leads into the unknown, will you choose to trust the King to guide your steps? Will you lay aside your own evaluation of the instruction in favor of dependence on the One who is giving the instruction? Far better if you do it before fifteen years have passed!

AN OLD THING

Brooke and I recently spent six days in Europe, celebrating our tenth wedding anniversary and returning to the place in London where we were engaged. Although the trip was mostly a chance to get away, we also toured some of the historic sites: Buckingham Palace, Westminster Abbey, Benjamin

Franklin's London house, and Christ's Church, to name just a few. While nearly all of these locations were beautiful, many of them were also in some state of decay. At first, it seemed natural that buildings so old would be starting to crumble. But the decay was not uniform—some buildings showed much greater signs of wear than others. As we read the accompanying placards, it struck me that while the age of a building certainly contributed to its condition, its durability was far more dependent on the quality of the original construction and the amount of care it had since received.

> When we perceive the new thing the King is doing, will we be bold enough to follow?

When a building is new, it generally receives careful attention. But as it ages, there is a temptation to neglect it, and over time the original beauty can become concealed and forgotten. This leads to decay. But if the design is timeless and the foundation is sure, the beauty remains and is concealed only by the dust of neglect that accumulates as time passes.

There are numerous parallels to our lives, but to me the most significant is the guidance this insight provides for how we should relate to people and events from our past as we step into the new thing—the eternal thing—the King has for us.

Our Design Is Timeless

First, we can stand on the assurance that our design is timeless. We were "fearfully and wonderfully" formed by skilled hands (Psalm 139:14). Our Creator instilled in us the specific talents and traits we would need to carry out His intended mission for our lives. So even if we have walked away from the King and show the visible signs of neglect in our souls, we can rest assured that a solid foundation remains. If we turn back to the King and commit to using our God-given abilities for him, our original purpose—service to the King—can still be found.

> The new thing you are called to build will likely be laid on a foundation that already exists.

Sure, it may take some work to reveal that beauty again, but rest assured it is still there. In fact, just as old buildings attract more tourists than new buildings, our design grows richer and more beautiful to our Maker, the King. The longer we walk in service to the King, the more He will lead us into new things He is doing and the greater our understanding of Him will become. This sustained relationship with the King begins to transition our pursuit of Him into a tangible discovery of Him.

We Can Build on Others' Foundations

Next, are we acknowledging the beautiful design and workmanship that exists in those who have walked before us?

Are we gleaning from their knowledge and wisdom? Or are we casting them aside as useless in favor of the latest and greatest?

As we consider how to successfully focus on the new thing we are called into, I suggest that the most productive way forward is building on the foundations of those who have walked before us. After all, the new path you are being called to is one that has almost certainly been trod before. The new thing you are called to build will likely be laid on a foundation that already exists.

Who has gone before you and is worthy of following in his or her footsteps?

What old foundations exist in your life that might serve as a launching point for your new thing?

Our pursuit of the King will certainly take us into new things He is doing. But as we walk in courage into those new things, we should make every effort to do it alongside those who have gone before us. We should honor the foundation they have laid, and we should shelter in the wisdom of their experience. If we are to be successful in our search for the King, we must heed the counsel of those who have pursued Him before us.

So as we learn to resist the urge to dwell on that which is in the past, let us not do it by rejecting the things of old. Let us do it in a way that builds upon them. Let us make the old thing new again.

THE ETERNAL KING REIGNS IN US

I want to make one final observation before leaving our discussion of following the Eternal King into a new thing, and it has to do with the passage in Matthew 25 we discussed in chapter 1. I challenge each of us to embrace the idea that, while our sins are fully forgiven and forgotten when we accept the King's atonement for them (Psalm 103:12), the things we do on this side of eternity have an eternal impact.

Theologians disagree about how to define the King's reign here on earth and whether or not to link it with His eternal reign. To be candid, I think the debate largely misses the point. To be sure, there is value in understanding the details about how the King will transition us into our eternal rest and communion with Him. But working out those details is the King's job. Meanwhile, we have very specific instructions to follow—instructions that, according to Matthew 25, have ramifications for all of eternity:

Feed the hungry.

Give water to the thirsty.

Befriend the outcast.

Clothe the naked.

Care for the afflicted.

Visit the prisoner.

Each of these acts will be counted as an act toward the King when we are called to account for our time here on earth. But they are more than that. They are also the visible evidence that our hearts have indeed been turned toward the King. They are the criteria that will be used to separate those who are found to be in the King (sheep) from those who are not (goats).

It is for this reason that the main challenge of this book is for each of us to choose a life of service to the King. Our intellectual search for the King yields essential head knowledge about who the King is and the role He wants to play in our lives. But in order for that intellectual understanding to be of real value, it has to transform our hearts. A true discovery of the King occurs when an intellectual understanding of Him takes root inside us. Once we have discovered the King in that intimate way, our hearts will be compelled to serve Him.

While salvation is indeed a free gift we accept by professing a genuine belief in Jesus, the King has called us to demonstrate that belief in specific ways during our lives on earth. Our service in the King's court will be on display on the day we enter the King's presence, standing as evidence of our true love for the King. Our service in the King's court will separate the sheep from the goats and will determine whether we truly believed.

I challenge you to embrace the fact that what you do today has a pivotal impact on the eternal kingdom. The King has a world to save. He has a globe full of individual souls, and He cares intimately for each of them.

Our lives are linked between this world and the next. Our actions here on earth will reverberate in the eternal kingdom. What eternal sound will we choose to set in motion today?

The King is doing a new thing. Do you perceive it?

CHAPTER FOUR
The King's Name

*Therefore God exalted him to the highest place
and gave him the name that is above every name.*

Philippians 2:9

W e are all Bennetts!"

It was a joyful discovery for our seven-year-old son, Jude. We were in the midst of a beach vacation with Papa and Gramma (my parents), my six siblings and their spouses, and all of the grandchildren. Jude, of course, understood that this was a vacation with family, and we had often discussed which ones were my brothers and sisters, and which ones were his cousins. But somehow lost in the translation of parent/child communication was the idea of association by name. Jude had not realized that every person present either was a Bennett, had once been a Bennett, was married to a Bennett, or was born to a Bennett. The discovery was cause for celebration for Jude—his cousins were Bennetts too! Even those who were called by another name were still Bennett cousins. It was too good to be true!

A name is a powerful thing. Association with a name is even more powerful. The act of giving someone your name, or the acceptance of someone else's name, is a timeless and public expression of association. It communicates value and a desire to share identity. In much of the world today, it means one of two things: connected by blood or specifically chosen.

A Blood Name

When a child is born, he or she takes the name of his or her parents. There is a blood connection that brings with it a shared name. The bond of blood is special. It is a bond that Brooke and I cannot adequately express in words as we relate to our children. The cliché "blood is thicker than water" underlines the point: a blood association is strong, meaningful, and instinctively cherished and defended.

A Chosen Name

There is also a name that is chosen. When two people take marriage vows, it is customary for the bride to take on the name of her husband. Similarly, when a child joins a family by adoption, he or she is given the name of the adopting family. In many ways, these bonds of name association are even more powerful than a blood bond, as they are a result of having been chosen.

The prophet Isaiah illustrates the concept of "chosen" brilliantly and repeatedly:

> But now listen, Jacob, my servant,
>   Israel, whom I have chosen.
> This is what the LORD says—
>   he who made you, who formed you in the womb,
>   and who will help you:

Do not be afraid, Jacob, my servant,
Jeshurun, whom I have chosen. (Isaiah 44:1–2)

Notice how the declaration of creation is bookended by reminders of having been chosen:

"My servant, Israel, *whom I have chosen . . .*"
". . . Jacob, my servant, Jeshurun, *whom I have chosen.*"

It is as though the King is saying, "Do not let the fact that you are My son detract from the fact that I have chosen you."

Isaiah 41:9 takes it to yet another level: "I took you from the ends of the earth, from its farthest corners I called you. I said, 'You are my servant'; *I have chosen you and have not rejected you.*"

The King of the universe easily could have chosen another way to be exalted. He could have orchestrated any or all of creation to sing His praise. In fact, Luke 19:40 reminds us that if our declaration of the King falls silent, even "the stones will cry out." The point is that He did not need you and me, save one reason: He desired you and me.

He *chose* you and me.

The King of the universe, who made you and formed

> The King
> of the universe,
> who made you
> and formed
> you, chose you.

you, chose you. In fact, He went out of His way to choose you. He went to the ends of the earth and to its farthest corners to find you. He calls you a child of the King.

After all of that, there is simply no cause to question our identity. There is no reason to doubt whose we are and where we belong.

After all, the King has given us His name!

But that is only the beginning. Once we understand that we share His name, it is time to move into action.

It is time for each of us to honestly assess who we are, and—more important—*whose* we are. The King has chosen to given us His name. He entangles His identity with each of us (a risky proposition, given His perfection and our decided lack of perfection). But because the King has chosen to reveal Himself through His people, a deeper knowledge of Him can be found by reflecting on several key questions.

WHAT IS MY NAME?

A name is significant because it often carries with it a mission. A name is more than just what we are called. It is what we are called to. It is an identity. In many cases our name is synonymous with our life's work. This is especially true when we take on the name of the King and enlist in His service.

The story of Abraham depicts this idea with clarity and poignancy. In Genesis 17, God appeared to Abram with an incredible promise that Abram would become the father of many nations. At the time, Abram was ninety-nine years old, and his wife, Sarai, was ninety. All of the evidence suggested that God issued this call too late or maybe confused Abram with someone else. At the very least, it was a suspicious mission to assign to Abram and Sarai.

> The King has chosen to given us His name.

The mission was so outrageous that Abram attempted to improve on God's plan by asking Him to fulfill His promise through his son Ishmael, who had been conceived with Sarai's servant Hagar in a desperate attempt to rush God's promise. The multigenerational chaos that ensued continues to impact geopolitical affairs today in a significant way. Abram desperately wanted to receive God's promise, but he did not have the faith to trust in God's plan to accomplish it.

When the King has called us to a specific purpose, there is no substitute for accomplishing that plan. There is no improving on the King's plan. When the King calls you, He has already equipped you for that which He is calling you to. In the case of Abram, this equipping came with a name change. Look at the way the King issued this charge to Abram:

> No longer will you be called Abram; your name will be Abraham, for I have made you a father of many nations. (Genesis 17:5)

Remember, Abram was ninety-nine years old. Abram was not the father of many nations, and he had no practical prospects whatsoever of becoming one. Yet God identified Abram not as the man he was but as the man God was moving him to be. He gave Abram a new name—Abraham—in order to stamp on him the promise that would be fulfilled. And God did not settle for saying, "I *will make* you the father of many nations"; instead, He used the past tense: "I *have made* you a father of many nations."

> The King identifies you as the person who will fulfill that which He has called you to.

You see, in God's eyes, it was already done. He had issued the promise, so the matter was sealed. Nothing could undo it, and only time stood between what was and what would be. And to prove it, God gave them new names: Abraham and Sarah.

WHERE SHOULD I GO?

What is the King calling you to? As our search begins to transition toward how to discover and respond to the King, it is critical for us to understand that the King identifies you as the person who will fulfill that which He has called you to. He has already given you a name—His name—that reflects His mission for your life. Further, He has already equipped you to live out that plan. When we look in the mirror, we see something far less than the King sees. We see our shortcomings and weaknesses. The King sees someone who was carefully crafted with individualized skills and characteristics to accomplish very specific tasks for Him. He sees someone perfectly suited for the journey He is calling us to.

But here is the catch. The person we see in the mirror must find the courage and the faith to take the journey that is set before us. Not only does that journey lead to the things the King would have us do, but it also makes us the person the King sees when we look in the mirror. We must receive the name that the King is proclaiming over us, and then we must walk in the mission that matches that name. The two are beautifully intertwined:

What is my name? *I am a child of the King, and I bear His name.*

Where should I go? *I will run to the King.*

AM I A SAINT OR A SINNER?

Our search for the King involves a pursuit of a greater knowledge of Him and a greater understanding of who we are in Him. If we are to truly move beyond a search for the King, and into a discovery of and service to the King, it is essential that we understand both of these components. We must know the face and character of the King, and we must understand our own identity within the King as well.

I have regularly contemplated the question of what it means to be a saint. By "saint," I do not mean a figure who is blameless. We sometimes elevate individuals to a standard of perfection, but Scripture clearly tells us that none has ever achieved that level (Romans 3:23). Rather, I want to know what it means to be a saint whose identity is found solely in the King, who is widely known to be in the service of the King, and who is able to walk through both success and trial and still be found in the King on the other side.

When considering which people I would place in this category, I think of the giants of the faith in the Bible, such as Moses, Noah, and Abraham. Likewise, in my life, I think of those who have won countless souls to a saving knowledge of the King. I think of those who have demonstrated great vision or leadership in a field that has advanced the kingdom cause. Or I think of those who are lesser known but have proven instrumental in my life. These are the ones who seem like saints to me. And in fact, I believe many of them are.

However, it is not what each of these has accomplished for the King that makes them a saint. It is also certainly not having a blameless life. I say that with confidence, because we know that no one—other than Jesus—has achieved perfection. So what is the common link? What is the secret sauce of sainthood? What is evident in the lives of each of these King followers that makes them saints rather than sinners?

I propose it is a conquering of sin. Notice I did not say the *absence* of sin—quite the contrary. Sin is evident in each of them (in some cases, vividly and painfully evident). But in each case, these saints have come to a point where they stopped running from their sin and faced it head-on. They dealt with it, and they conquered it. Yes, in some cases, that made the sin more public. But in many cases, the very act of addressing their sin stripped the sin of its power in their lives. It was what allowed them to gain victory over it.

> A saint is nothing but a conquering sinner.

You see, if we desire sainthood, we must first come to a realization that we have fallen short and are powerless over sin in our own strength. But that is not an admission of defeat. In fact, it is the key to victory, because it gives us access to a power that conquers all sin. It gives us freedom to declare ourselves pure and blameless—not because of what we have (or have not) done but because we have acknowledged our shortcomings and our need for the King's mercy.

It is not the absence of sin that makes a saint; it is the conquering of sin. And in order to conquer sin, we must be willing to turn into it and face it head-on.

A saint is nothing but a conquering sinner.

THE NAME ABOVE ALL NAMES

From a very young age, had you asked me what I wanted to be when I grew up, I would have said either a Major League Baseball player for the Chicago Cubs or the play-by-play radio announcer for the Chicago Cubs. That was what I wanted to do with my life, or at least so I thought. As it turns out, the King had other plans. I was a reasonably solid baseball player, but nowhere near good enough to make a profession out of it. Add in a knee surgery, a shoulder surgery, and a bit of age, and it takes bailing wire just to roll me out for church softball games!

Whether it is a professional athlete, a doctor, a lawyer, or any other profession, it is natural to have desires about who we will be and what we will become. Although our desires may change over time, there are always pursuits that catch our eye. Many of these pursuits are perfectly noble, worthy of our attention, and possibly even a part of the King's plan for our service to Him. After all, we know that He is inclined to accomplish His will using the desires of our hearts (Psalm 37:4).

> Are we looking to make a name for ourselves, or lifting high the Name above all names?

But remember this: you and I can truly possess only one name.

There might be any number of pursuits for you to engage in during the course of your life, but the reality is that you will do them under the banner of the name you have chosen.

Many will choose their own names, and make fame or personal fortune their primary mission.

Many will choose the name of power and influence, and

use a political office or a business achievement to acquire even more influence.

Some, like my childhood self, will choose the name of athletic achievement, and will dedicate their lives to feats of physical strength and ability.

Others will dedicate themselves to the classroom and will acquire more knowledge of the world than those around them.

Your own name. Fame. Wealth. Power. Influence. Athletic achievement. Academic excellence.

The choices are endless, and each of them is a perfectly fine pursuit if indeed it is where the King would have you serve. I am blessed to know heroes of faith in the fields of business, politics, athletics, and academics. These pursuits can be noble. The question is, are we looking to make a name for ourselves, or lifting high the Name above all names? Are we making these pursuits into false kings, or are we using them to the glory of the King of kings?

There are many names we can take on, but there is only one name that leads to true service in the King's court. One name that moves you from chasing your own dreams to discovering the depths of all that the King has for you. One name that is above all others.

It is the royal name. It is the King's name. And it is the name that has been freely offered to you and to me. Let us take on that name and make it our singular pursuit.

CHAPTER FIVE

The King Who Walks with Us

Enoch walked faithfully with God;
then he was no more,
because God took him away.

Genesis 5:24

As we grow in our knowledge of the King, the pursuit to know Him more takes on a different look and feel. It becomes less academic. It becomes less head and more heart, less searching and more discovery. In a word, the pursuit of the King becomes a *verb*. For those who find the answer to the question, "Who is the King?" there is a stunning realization that the longing in their souls was not simply to know the King. Their longing was to *walk* with the King.

TWO PEOPLE
WHO WALKED WITH GOD

The phrase *walked with God* is frequently used among Christians but is found rather sparingly in Scripture. There are many places where some might infer that God walked with a person (for example, Adam and Eve in Genesis 3:8). But I find only two instances where it is stated as plain fact. Each of these examples is worth a closer look.

Noah

Genesis 6:9 describes Noah as "a righteous man, blameless among the people of his time, and *he walked faithfully with God.*" We will explore the story of Noah and his service to the King in a later chapter, but for now, it is important to understand the context in which Noah is described as having "walked faithfully with God." In short, God had searched the world for men and women of righteousness, and He had come up so empty that He decided to destroy the world with a flood and start over. That is how desperate the situation was—the almighty King, "not wanting anyone to perish" (2 Peter 3:9), decided to destroy the earth and start over.

"How would He start over?" you ask. He would use the one man He found walking with Him. The fresh start could have certainly involved the creation of a new "first" man and woman, but instead the King used a man who proved he knew how to walk with Him in the most desperate of times.

Enoch

Enoch appears only briefly and in only a few places in Scripture,[1] yet his legacy is in many ways unmatched.

First, in Luke 3:37, we see that Jesus the King is a descendant of Enoch. The lineage of Jesus is something that Scripture repeatedly declares as intentional and significant. The Father carefully chose to send His Son into the world through a very specific set of people. These people were certainly not flawless, but all were a part of the carefully orchestrated arrival of the King of kings.

Next, Enoch appears in the famous "Heroes of Faith" chapter, Hebrews 11. Here is the epitaph of Enoch:

By faith Enoch was taken from this life, so that he did not experience death: "He could not be found, because God had taken him away." For before he was taken, he was commended as one who pleased God. And without faith it is impossible to please God, because anyone who comes to him must believe that he exists and that he rewards those who earnestly seek him. (vv. 5–6)

It is "appointed unto men once to die" (Hebrews 9:27 KJV), but Enoch did not taste death. Enoch knew an intimacy with God that was so deep it allowed him to escape the bonds of earth and death. The Father so enjoyed the company of Enoch that He called Enoch to His side, bypassing the avenue of physical death.

The reason for God's pleasure with Enoch and His urgency to have Enoch by His side is summed up as *faith*. But countless people in Scripture—including many heroes in Hebrews 11—are described as having *great faith*. So what made Enoch different? What made his relationship with God stand apart? I believe the answer is alluded to at the end of the passage, where it is stated that God "rewards those who earnestly seek him." A closer look at the brief Old Testament description of Enoch's life underscores this point. In a word, Enoch circumvented death and was taken to the Father's side because he walked with God.

The description of Enoch's life is brief, and it is worth reading carefully:

> When Jared had lived 162 years, he became the father of Enoch. After he became the father of Enoch, Jared lived 800 years and had other sons and daughters. Altogether, Jared lived a total of 962 years, and then he died.
>
> When Enoch had lived 65 years, he became the father of Methuselah. After he became the father of Methuselah, Enoch walked faithfully with God 300 years and had other sons and daughters. Altogether, Enoch lived a total of 365 years. *Enoch walked faithfully with God*; then he was no more, because God took him away. (Genesis 5:18–24)

Enoch "walked faithfully with God; then he was no more, because God took him away." There is *faithful*, and then there is *walking faithfully*. It is a worthy and noble goal to be faithful. I long to be found faithful on the day I stand before the Eternal King on His throne. It is a label that is worth pursuing unto death.

But what if we have an opportunity to go beyond faithful?

What if we, like Enoch, could be found to have *walked faithfully*? What if we could know an intimacy with the King that ushers in a personal discovery of Him? I believe with all my heart that Scripture promises just that opportunity. I believe each of us is called to experience the King in the way Enoch did. And while Enoch's dramatic detour around death is phenomenal and instructive about how deeply the King longs for this kind of intimacy with us, do not let it distract you from the real goal—that of *walking faithfully with our King*.

I am also struck by the wording of the description of Enoch's 365 years of life. Enoch's first 65 years—before the birth of his son, Methuselah—are twice noted with relative dismissiveness. Scripture simply says, "When Enoch had lived 65 years," and then after a more detailed description of the next 300 years, "Altogether, Enoch lived a total of 365 years." It is difficult to say conclusively what those first 65 years of Enoch's life were like. But I can tell you

> There is *faithful*, and then there is *walking faithfully*.

with authority what happened in the next 300 years! "After he became the father of Methuselah, Enoch walked faithfully with God 300 years. . . . Enoch walked faithfully with God; then he was no more, because God took him away."

Something changed in Enoch's life about the time Methuselah was born. And while the description of this shift is brief, we can conclude with great confidence that it was the result of a greater and a more active intimacy with Enoch's Creator. Whatever the cause for the shift, when Enoch was sixty-five he began to transition into an active discovery of the King. In short, Enoch began to truly walk with God.

This was no stroll around the block either! Enoch walked faithfully with God for *three hundred years*! If my measure of having walked faithfully were taken, what unit of measurement would be used? Weeks? Days? Hours? Maybe even minutes? What about you? Can you lay claim to having walked faithfully with the King for even one year of your life? Have you experienced what it means to know the King so intimately that you are aware of His desire for you at every moment of every day? I ask not out of condemnation, but with a desperate plea for each of us to long for exactly that kind of walk with the King.

> Have you experienced what it means to know the King so intimately that you are aware of His desire for you at every moment of every day?

Something clicked when Enoch was sixty-five. It seems likely this change was triggered by the birth of his son, Methuselah. But either way, Enoch grasped hold of the truth that his pursuit of God was simply not enough. Upon reaching this conclusion, he laid aside pursuit in favor of discovery. And then he walked in that discovery for three hundred years. No wonder the King finally took him! Enoch had discovered that it was not enough for him to know the King. Enoch had developed an insatiable desire to *walk faithfully* with the King. He did just that for three hundred years, and then he was no more. Enoch's three hundred years of walking had earned him a passage into eternity that was unparalleled—both before that time and since.

We may not slip the bonds of death in the way that Enoch did (though we can certainly slip the bonds of a permanent death in favor of eternal life). But Enoch's faithful walk with the King is still available to us today. The King is searching for those who will walk faithfully with Him.

"*Who is the King?*" He is the One who walks with us.

WHO IS THE KING TO ME?

As we seek to walk faithfully with the King, it is necessary to reflect on what we know about the King's character and personality. It is instructive to consider the many roles the King plays in our lives—those of Savior, Lord, Master, Friend, Advocate, and many more. We will explore these roles in order to solidify our understanding of how involved He desires to be in our lives.

But even as we look at the various roles the King plays, it is important that we remember the precious truth that He plays these roles not as some far-off, detached figment of our imaginations, but rather as the One who journeys beside us and longs for interaction with us. He is not a king on some distant mountaintop or hiding away in some castle ruling over his subjects, but rather He is laid low among us in order to be discovered by us.

I am reminded of one of my most vivid childhood memories. My youngest sister, Holly, and I took a road trip with Grandpa and Grandma. It was just the four of us, which was special in and of itself because Grandpa and Grandma had oodles and oodles of grandchildren, and they have even more today! So Grandpa and Grandma were always taking grandchildren on vacations with them, which is a huge testament of their self-sacrificing love. On this particular occasion, a nineteen-year-old Thann and an eight-year-old Holly sat in the back of the old station wagon as Grandpa drove and Grandma handed out bottomless snacks. We drove 5,473 miles (Grandpa and Grandma keep meticulous records of these things) from Illinois to California and back over a two-week stretch, and the beauty of the trip was in two things: (1) the number of destinations, and (2) the fact that the focus was more on the journey than the destinations.

Our turning-around point was my older sister's apartment in Fresno, California, where we stayed for a few days before starting home. But Fresno was not really the destination. It was simply the most westward stop among many destinations. I remember staying in cheap, roadside motels and waking up the next morning to the smell of coffee and the sight of Grandpa with a map and a question: "Where should we go today?" My grandpa and grandma are planners, and I suspect they knew good and well where we should go, but they wanted our input. They wanted the trip to be about more than where we ended up and instead about how we went about getting there. They wanted it to be about discovery.

So we stopped and saw everything from the Grand Canyon to Four Corners to hole-in-the-wall, greasy-spoon eateries. I remember one particular stop at a rocky formation along the side of the highway. As far as I know, the rocky formation does not even have a name, and I would not be able to find it again if I tried. But Holly and I saw it as we were driving past and decided we wanted to climb it. I suspect we were motivated mainly by the opportunity to get out of the car and stretch our legs, but whatever the reason, we asked to stop and climb the rocks. So Grandpa stopped and Holly and I climbed the rocks. I still remember standing on top of that rocky hill with my little sister and looking down at Grandpa and Grandma at the bottom of the hill. The randomness of it made it a memory. The discovery of something unique alongside someone I loved made it special. It is a feeling that all too often escapes us in this busy world, but it illustrates how the King wants to be discovered by us. He is not interested in being found at our turning-around point; He wants to be discovered in the everyday moments as we walk with Him.

So as we consider the King's role in our lives and ask the question, "Who is the King to me?" let us focus on those last two words: *to me*. Let us reflect on the character of the King, but let us do it in a way that moves us from an abstract view of a distant King and toward a realization that the King is all of these things *to us specifically.* His relationship with each of us is unique and personal, and He embodies each of these characteristics for the purpose of *engaging in discovery alongside us.*

> We are inundated with options of royalty to serve. But there is only one King who is also the Savior of our souls.

So it is not simply, "Who is the King?" but rather, "Who is the King to me?"

The King Is My Savior

"There is no God apart from me, a righteous God and a Savior; there is none but me" (Isaiah 45:21).

This world offers many kings from which to choose. We are inundated with options of royalty to serve. But there is only one King who is also the Savior of our souls. There is only one King who came to "seek and to save" (Luke 19:10). The discovery of that King will require the laying aside of other kings.

The King is Savior to me, and there is none but Him.

The King Is My Lord

"You alone are the LORD. You made the heavens, even the highest heavens, and all their starry host, the earth and all that is on it, the seas and all that is in them. You give life to everything, and the multitudes of heaven worship you" (Nehemiah 9:6).

We often serve so many things. We serve earthly pursuits. We serve our desires. We serve things that were created. But we are called to serve the Creator. We are called to serve the one, true Lord. Lordship can be a difficult concept for our human flesh, but it is only through submission to His authority over our lives that we can walk in true and free discovery of Him.

The King is Lord to me, and I will worship Him alone.

The King Is My Master

"No one can serve two masters. Either you will hate the one and love the other, or you will be devoted to the one and despise the other. You cannot serve both God and money" (Matthew 6:24).

One of the enemy's favorite lies is, "You do not have to choose." In fact, it is the original lie he used on Eve when he assured her that God surely did not really mean for anything to be off-limits. But in fact, God meant exactly that. However, it was not even about the fruit, but rather about the fact that God was calling on Adam and Eve to *choose Him.* The existence of other masters presents us with a choice. But we cannot have both. We must choose between the masters of this world and the Master who transcends this world.

The King is Master to me, and I choose to serve Him alone.

The King Is My Advocate

"If anybody does sin, we have an advocate with the Father— Jesus Christ, the Righteous One" (1 John 2:1).

We have all sinned and fallen short (Romans 3:23). This is not a statement of defeat. In fact, it is precisely the opposite. It is an acknowledgment of our weakness, coupled with a declaration of dependence. It is an admission of our need for an Advocate, linked to the King's promise of our defense. He has paid the price for our failure in advance, and as if that were not enough, He goes before us to plead our case. Because the King has intervened and taken up our cause, we can approach the Father as "blameless" and "without blemish" (Ephesians 5:27; Colossians 1:22), our sins removed "as far as the east is from the west" (Psalm 103:12).

The King is an Advocate to (and for) me, and He will intervene for me.

The King Is My Friend

"There is a friend who sticks closer than a brother" (Proverbs 18:24).

We are conditioned to believe that a Savior, Lord, Master, and King cannot also be our friend. We are used to the human condition, which suggests that anyone we pledge servitude to cannot be fully trusted and might take advantage of us. But this is no ordinary human king we serve. We serve *the* King, who is worthy of our praise and service. But that same King can be trusted with an intimate knowledge of our imperfect and fallen selves. Our King is not waiting to catch us in our imperfections but is waiting as a friend to help us through them.

> We must choose between the masters of this world and the Master who transcends this world.

The King is a friend to me, and He sticks closer than a brother.

WALK FAITHFULLY

It is a wonderful thing to know our King. But we will never fully know Him if we continue to pursue Him as though He is nothing more than an intellectual destination. If we are to experience the King in all of His many roles—including Savior, Lord, Master, Advocate, and Friend—we must learn what it means to transition from a search for the King into a daily discovery of Him.

Let us not be satisfied with the attributes of the King we have experienced to this point. May we recognize what

Enoch did at age sixty-five—that there is a deeper level of intimacy with the King available to us.

Knowledge of the King is a solid foundation. But let us not stop there. As we will learn in part 2, we must build on that foundation with a true discovery of Him. May it be the deepest desire of our hearts to walk faithfully with Him.

PART TWO

Discover the King

CHAPTER SIX

Discovery over Pursuit

*You will seek me and find me
when you seek me with all your heart.*

Jeremiah 29:13

Whenever I hear the word *seek*, I am reminded of the "Kick the Can" game we played on our rural Illinois property as kids. Mind you, our version of "Kick the Can" was not your standard hide-and-seek. This was a team hide-and-seek game played with at least a dozen players on a two-and-a-half-acre playing field, with the goal of sneaking past enemy lines to kick the can and win the game. Oh, and one other small detail: we played it well after dark. The darker, the better. All the outside lights would be turned off, and as many of the indoor lights as Dad and Mom would allow as well. Let me tell you, it gets dark at night in the country! Especially when you are a child with a healthy imagination.

The darkness, however, turned an ordinary game into an exhilarating adventure. Our property was full of giant oak trees—trees that managed to cast shadows on even the darkest of nights. Some nights it was possible to lie down in the grass within one of those shadows and be virtually un-detectable unless someone from the other team tripped over you. Lying there as your pursuer walked mere feet away was exhilarating. However, when you became the pursuing team, it was disconcerting to say the least to know that a dozen pairs of hidden eyes were watching your every move and waiting for the opportunity to rise from the shadows and bolt past you in pursuit of the can.

I remember one cool, fall evening when Uncle Tom and a bunch of our cousins were playing. It was a particularly dark night, and Uncle Tom was, in my opinion, the greatest player our little game ever produced. He was fast, quick, sneaky, and most importantly, conniving. Uncle Tom cared less about the objective of the game—kicking the can—and more about putting the other team on edge. Uncle Tom loved it when his pursuers felt uneasy.

On this particular night, when it was their turn to hide, Uncle Tom took his entire team to the back edge of our property, where there were no trees or true cover but simply a slight downslope before our property ended and the already-harvested cornfield began. Uncle Tom and his team lay facedown in the shadow of that gentle slope and waited.

And they waited.

And they waited.

My team must have looked for Uncle Tom's team for an hour. We could not find a single person. We checked behind every tree, bush, and structure. We walked by every shadow (so we thought), and even checked every vehicle in the driveway (which were off-limits, but after a certain point, we were sure Uncle Tom was cheating). Eventually we sent someone to go check inside the house to see if they had abandoned the game without telling us.

There were many moments where any one of them could have simply stood up, run to the can, and kicked it to win the game. But instead, they waited.

I believe they waited because Uncle Tom wanted something more than simply winning the game. Uncle Tom wanted to create a memory. He wanted to create a moment we would remember twenty-five years later. That was infinitely more valuable to him than winning a child's game.

I will never forget how far my heart dropped when I finally bumped into Uncle Tom as he lay in the grass on that gentle slope. The result was that my team "won" the game, but all of us knew who had really won, and I am willing to wager that every cousin who was there that night remembers the time when they either hid with Uncle Tom on that slope, or they hunted for Uncle Tom and his team on that slope.

The memory is ingrained because it is unique. It is ingrained because it triggered not just our minds but our emotions and adrenaline as well. And it is ingrained because it generated a touch of fear. It was memorable because it was a shared experience that involved the heart. It was not simply an academic exercise or a classroom experience—it was a discovery. It was something that each of us acquired, but we did so together.

I truly believe that is what God means when He says, "You will seek me and find me when you seek me with all your heart" (Jeremiah 29:13). This verse invites us to a discovery of the King that goes well beyond a quiet time or a mental understanding of the King. Both of those pursuits are certainly vital to our walk with the King, but it is also where we all too often stop. We pursue the King, but we stop short of engaging in situations where we are able to discover Him. We avoid situations that lead us into the shadows on the edge of the property and involve a touch of uncertainty and fear. We are afraid of what will happen if we are alone in that place and in that moment. We are afraid of bumping into the unknown, and because of our fear, we forfeit the possibility of bumping into the King.

We do not trust that the King will meet us there, and so we do not discover.

Let us decide that we will no longer settle for only a head knowledge of our King. No longer will we stop once we can recite what the King has instructed and called us to. No longer will we be afraid of the shadows or the unknown. No longer will we be content without discovery. It is time for you, and for me, to engage our full hearts in our pursuit of the King. It is time we step out and discover that the full face of the King cannot be known unless we are engaging our full being in the discovery of Him.

Our minds must be engaged.

Our bodies must be active.

Our hearts must be committed.

The King is waiting. He desires every part of us, and in an effort to draw our complete being to Him, He continues to wait. Make no mistake about it—He will meet you in that place of daring adventure, and you will discover Him. But He will remain hidden until you decide to discover Him with your whole heart.

WHOM DO I PROCLAIM?

On February 13, 2016, United States Supreme Court Justice Antonin Scalia died. Justice Scalia's death was newsworthy for a number of reasons, not the least of which was the political fight that ensued to fill his vacant seat on the Court. Justice Scalia had been a leading conservative voice on a Court that had long been closely divided along ideological lines. As such, Justice Scalia's time on the Court made him a polarizing figure for many. Politicos on all sides viewed his death as an opportunity to swing the balance of the Court toward their preferred ideological position. In so many ways, it was a travesty for the passing of a man of such significance to trigger such a contentious political fight.

> We are afraid of bumping into the unknown, and because of our fear, we forfeit the possibility of bumping into the King.

Justice Scalia's funeral was held at the famous Basilica of the National Shrine of the Immaculate Conception. I watched the service on TV. But it was the homily given by Justice Scalia's son, Father Paul Scalia, that stopped me in my tracks.

Father Scalia, stoic but visibly affected by the loss of his father, took to the lectern and began with these words: "We are gathered here because of one man. A man known personally to many of us, known only by reputation to even more; a man loved by many, scorned by others; a man known for great controversy, and for great compassion."

Those of us listening recognized it as an appropriate description of his father's reputation. The gathering was, indeed, to celebrate Justice Scalia's life. Or at least so we thought.

> Our willingness to declare the name of the King is central to our discovery of Him.

Father Scalia continued, "That man, of course, is Jesus of Nazareth."

With one sentence, Father Scalia reminded me, and everyone else listening, that the mass should not really be about Justice Scalia. It should be about the King.

Father Scalia concluded his opening with, "It is He whom we proclaim."[1]

The entire opening was all of three sentences. It took maybe fifteen seconds. And yet I have not been able to shake the impact of his words. First, it was extraordinarily powerful for a son to use the opportunity of his father's funeral to remind us that everything and every day should be a celebration of the King. Even more powerful was Father Scalia's determination to proclaim the name of the King, even in a moment where nobody would have faulted him for reminiscing about his father. Father Scalia was not content for the service to be only about his father, but rather insisted on proclaiming the name of the King. The King is revered by many and scorned by many, but the pressing matter for Father Scalia was to proclaim His name.

Whom do you and I proclaim? In difficult times, or moments when we have every justification for a selfish focus, do we still proclaim the King? Our willingness to declare the name of the King is central to our discovery of Him. It must become our singular and ever-present passion!

HIS WORDS IN YOUR MOUTH

We so often doubt our ability to answer the King's call. When the King called the prophet Jeremiah into His service, Jeremiah did not believe he was capable of fulfilling the task. So the King professed intimate knowledge of Jeremiah and proclaimed that he had been created and set aside specifically for this task: "Before I formed you in the womb I knew you, before you were born I set you apart; I appointed you as a prophet to the nations" (Jeremiah 1:5).

I often doubt that I am equipped for the things the King has called me to. I easily forget that He has known me since before I was born and has placed within me everything needed for the tasks He has set out for me.

Jeremiah explained to God what seemed to be a valid reason for turning down the appointment he was being given: "'Alas, Sovereign LORD,' I said, 'I do not know how to speak; I am too young'" (v. 6).

Surely the ideal candidate to be a prophet to the nations would have powerful oratory skills and a voice that commands attention. Jeremiah had neither. So he confessed his hesitation to the King.

Our family knows a bit about difficulty forming words and the challenges that can stem from that difficulty. Our oldest child, Jude, is my best buddy in the world. Every night when I turn out the lights in his room, we remind each other of that by saying, "Best buddies forever!" I believe with every fiber in my being that Jude is fearfully and wonderfully made with the precise skill set he needs to fulfill the King's call on His life. This has been confirmed to me in a number of ways, and I am confident that he will do mighty things for the King.

Jude is also a bit like Jeremiah. Jude has been diagnosed with several developmental speech challenges. Included in these challenges is something called *apraxia*, which is an inability to physically form the sounds that make up the building blocks of language. It can be overcome, and Jude is working hard to do just that. But Jude faces some challenges as he interacts with the world. Just a few days ago, Jude was finishing soccer practice with his team when I heard several of the boys wildly jeering at Jude's pronunciation of a word. Now, maybe those boys didn't mean to be cruel, as these were seven-year-olds who did not grasp the reality of Jude's challenges. But my heart broke for Jude as he was forced to endure ridicule he did not deserve. As any parent will understand, I wanted to intervene and stop the pain.

But Jude did not need my intervention, and his simple response spoke volumes more than my intervention ever could. He simply shrugged and said, "Yeah, I don't speak so well . . . but I'm working on it!" It was a simple acknowledgment of reality and an equally simple profession that he is doing what he can to meet the challenge. My heart burst with gratitude for my best buddy's response to a difficult situation. He dealt with it much better than I would have.

Later that night, I was prompted to share this story from Jeremiah with Jude. I wanted to remind him that we all have our challenges, and the King's call on our lives often flows directly from those challenges. So I told him about Jeremiah's call to speak to the nations despite his poor communication skills. I told him about Jeremiah's understandable objection to that call. And then I told him about the King's response:

But the LORD said to me, "Do not say, 'I am too young.' You must go to everyone I send you to and say whatever I command you. Do not be afraid of them, for I am with you and will rescue you," declares the LORD.

Then the LORD reached out his hand and touched my mouth and said to me, "I have put my words in your mouth." (Jeremiah 1:7–9)

I have put My words in your mouth.

Whether it is speaking to the nations or some other task, our service to the King will only have its intended impact if it is conducted within the power and ability of the King. If we try to undertake our task in our own strength, it will fail. The King often chooses to use our areas of natural weakness to magnify the fact that it is His power at work in us that makes the difference.

> Rather than focus on your own abilities, focus on proclaiming the name of the One who called you.

Jeremiah did not need eloquence. Jude does not need eloquence. You and I do not need eloquence. But we must be willing to speak on behalf of the King. The King will put His words in our mouths.

I challenge you to resist the temptation to inventory your abilities in response to the King's call on your life. Certainly there is wisdom in using the skills the King has bestowed on you, but if you have been called to a specific task, neither your age nor your challenges should dissuade you from obeying.

If you have been called, rather than focus on your own abilities, focus on proclaiming the name of the One who called you. When you proclaim the King, He will fill your mouth with His words.

I cannot wait to witness what the King will do through Jude—and what He will do through you.

TAKE CRAZY TO THE GRAVE

It is one thing to appear crazy for a moment when you know redemption of your reputation is coming soon. But there are times where we must speak for the King—and yes, even appear a fool for the King—without any assurance that our reputation will be made whole. Those moments force us to consider whether we are willing to look foolish for the King to the end. Are we willing to take crazy to the grave?

The King did that for us.

In John 2, immediately after Jesus had driven the money changers from the temple, He was challenged by the religious leaders: "What sign can you show us to prove your authority to do all this?" (v. 18). The religious leaders were no doubt furious about what Jesus had done to the money changers, and Jesus's response would determine His fate. But it would also do something else—it would serve as evidence for or against Jesus's sanity. Think about it for a moment—if a man claiming to be the Son of God fashioned a weapon and used it to drive people from your church or place of worship, what would you think? I am certain I would believe that man to be insane and a threat to society. I am certain I would call for that man to be taken into custody. That is what Jesus did and was the backdrop against which He was being asked to show a sign to demonstrate His authority. His answer to this question would be His chance to salvage His reputation and save Himself from certain trouble.

Instead, Jesus decided to double down on crazy:

> Jesus answered them, "Destroy this temple, and I will raise it again in three days."
>
> They replied, "It has taken forty-six years to build this temple, and you are going to raise it in three days?" But the temple he had spoken of was his body. After he was raised from the dead, his disciples recalled what he had said. Then they believed the scripture and the words that Jesus had spoken. (vv. 19–22)

Jesus's response was crazy on so many levels. First, He was in hot water for causing a scene in the temple, so He excused His actions by suggesting the temple be torn down altogether! That was not exactly a sound strategy for exonerating Himself. Next, He used an allegory that was lost on those to whom He was speaking. The temple Jesus was referring to was not the physical building the religious leaders were concerned about, but rather His own body. Had Jesus clarified this point for them, it would have done much to defuse the situation. But Jesus let the misunderstanding carry. He let the meaning of His words be lost for the moment. He willingly donned the label of crazy.

Finally, in what I think is the most astonishing part of all, Jesus willingly accepted the label of crazy in a way that even His disciples would not understand until after He died. He chose words that almost certainly left even them shaking their heads and wondering about the sanity of their Messiah.

Jesus took on crazy, and He took it on all the way to the grave. I submit that He did so to demonstrate not just the authority by which He was acting in the temple but also the authority by which He would rise again in an act that conquered sin and death. Jesus was seeking a long-term impact with His response. He was pursuing the eternal impact that His words would have once their meaning was revealed as a result of His actions. But in order to achieve that end, He had to appear crazy. Further, He had to take that crazy to the grave.

> Jesus took on crazy, and He took it on all the way to the grave.

Is there an area of your life where you need to take on crazy? Is there something you feel called to do but are hesitant to take on because of what it will do to your reputation?

If we truly desire a discovery of the King, it just might require taking on crazy, and then taking that crazy to the grave! The result will be a justification from the lips of the King that will echo into eternity: "Whoever acknowledges me before others, I will also acknowledge before my Father in heaven" (Matthew 10:32).

> It is time to engage our full being—mind, body, and heart—in the active discovery of our King.

It is time for each us to refuse to settle for a pursuit of the King that stops short of discovery. It is time to engage our full being—mind, body, and heart—in the active discovery of our King. It is time to overcome our fear and step into the shadows He is calling us to illuminate. It is time to proclaim the name of the King. And yes, it is time to be willing to look crazy and appear a fool (1 Corinthians 4:10) if that is what it takes to discover Him. We have no reason to fear, because as we boldly step from pursuit into discovery and express a desire to proclaim His name, the King whispers, "I have put My words in your mouth."

CHAPTER SEVEN
A Voice in the Wilderness

"I am the voice of one calling in the wilderness,
'Make straight the way for the Lord.'"

John 1:23

The shift from the pursuit of the King to the active discovery of Him usually occurs in moments of testing. It happens when our theoretical knowledge of the King is challenged or stretched, and we are forced either to walk forward in faith or to remain content where we are. It is in these moments that we have the opportunity to truly discover the King by dialoguing with Him and allowing Him to be an active participant in our everyday life.

To properly respond to these pivotal challenges, we must draw on more than a head knowledge of the King. Rather, we must respond from a deeper, more intimate place in our hearts. And because the condition of our hearts is revealed by the things we say (Luke 6:45; Matthew 12:34), it is particularly important for us to evaluate how we are using our voices.

There may be no better case study for how to convert a head knowledge of the King into a heart knowledge of Him—and how that conversion is evidenced by the voice—than John the Baptist. Of course, John had the advantage of actually encountering the King in human form. That makes transitioning from an intellectual understanding to a life of practical application a bit easier! Still, John the Baptist faced significant challenges to his discovery of the King, and his example is instructive to all of us.

TESTING

Most of us know John the Baptist as a giant of faith who baptized Jesus and many others in the Jordan River. We know him as a great follower of Jesus. But he had to navigate a crossroads where many believed he was actually the Messiah. John had to successfully traverse the tricky terrain of human adulation and adoring praise. There are many lessons to take from John's life, but we will start with one that occurred before Jesus was even on the scene.

In John 1, John declared the imminent coming of the Lord. John was clear that he himself was not the Messiah; he was simply proclaiming the Messiah's impending arrival: "This is the one I spoke about when I said, 'He who comes after me has surpassed me because he was before me'" (John 1:15). Even so, many people surrounding John began to believe that he was the long-awaited Messiah. I have little doubt this occurred in large part because the power and authority of the King were flowing through John. Regardless, people began to proclaim John as a deity.

Now this was John's testimony when the Jewish leaders in Jerusalem sent priests and Levites to ask him who he was. He did not fail to confess, but confessed freely, "I am not the Messiah."

They asked him, "Then who are you? Are you Elijah?"

He said, "I am not."

"Are you the Prophet?"

He answered, "No."

Finally they said, "Who are you? Give us an answer to take back to those who sent us. What do you say about yourself?"

John replied in the words of Isaiah the prophet, "I am the voice of one calling in the wilderness, 'Make straight the way for the Lord.'"

Now the Pharisees who had been sent questioned him, "Why then do you baptize if you are not the Messiah, nor Elijah, nor the Prophet?"

"I baptize with water," John replied, "but among you stands one you do not know. He is the one who comes after me, the straps of whose sandals I am not worthy to untie." (vv. 19–27)

Essentially, the religious leaders of the land came to test John. They came asking if he was the Christ or the Prophet. They challenged John's commitment to humbling himself under the authority of the King. I think they expected to hear John profess he was a big shot, as evidenced by the crowds following him. The religious leaders had ill intentions, and they came with the tried-and-true approach of appealing to John's ego. They proposed that John should take on the mantle of the One he was proclaiming. It was a heady suggestion but also a dangerous one, because accepting it would have undermined the very reason for John's witness.

John defused the ploy by responding to the question "Who are you?" in this way: "I am A VOICE OF ONE CRYING IN THE WILDERNESS, 'MAKE STRAIGHT THE WAY OF THE LORD' as Isaiah the prophet said" (v. 23 NASB).

Oh, to be like John! John's response at this critical crossroads in his life demonstrated a deep longing to simply be a voice that speaks his message that points to the King, and he did it without regard for who was listening. His answer flowed from a heart that was committed to discovering the King.

POINTING ONLY TO THE KING

John's answer foiled the plans of the religious leaders. But when I read John's response, I see three strategies we can use in our own lives when we are tempted to accept the idea that we are to be more than a voice in the wilderness. Each of these strategies positions our hearts in way that allows a greater discovery of the King.

First, John's answer humbled himself. He openly acknowledged his own human limitations and rejected the idea of his own deity. He did not claim part of the mantle of leadership. Rather, he reiterated that the only reason for his existence was to prepare the way of his Master. The One they were looking for was yet to come!

Next, and similarly, John's response pointed only to the Christ. He rejected the assertion that his message was in any way about himself. It was only about the King. The same should be true for us. We are blessed beyond measure to have been called into the King's story. We have been invited into royalty as sons and daughters of the King, but the story is still about the King. The message we proclaim must be about Him, and Him alone. We must resist the urge to make it about us.

> We have been invited into royalty as sons and daughters of the King, but the story is still about the King.

Finally, John's answer was validated with the words of those who had gone before him. His quote from the prophet insulated his response from attack or critique, because the religious leaders did not want to come against the words of Isaiah. So often—even by way of our zeal to be a part of proclaiming the King—we compete with one another rather than support one another. We look to be heard over others who are also proclaiming the King rather than support each other in the effort. Sometimes we go so far as to discredit others who are proclaiming the King in a different (but valid) way. John rejected that temptation and instead stood on the authority of the faithful who had gone before him. This is an example we would do well to follow.

In two short sentences, John humbled himself, pointed only to the King, and reaffirmed the words of the prophet Isaiah. Again I say, "Oh, to be like John!" But John's answer, while brilliant in its humble defusing of the Pharisees' trap, would have to be backed up with action. It would be tested. John's response to that test would enable his discovery of the King.

LOSING INFLUENCE
TO ADVANCE THE KING

We live in a world where the size of our platform is important. The size of our churches, the reach of our voices, and the scope of our readership dictate our influence. If you want to know the clout of a person's online reach, it can be found with a few clicks to discover the number of followers on Facebook, Twitter, or Instagram. In total, this is a very positive thing. We have been given the magnificent ability to reach countless people for the King in this way—and with a little creativity, we can grow our platform for the King in ways never imagined just a generation ago.

Even so, one of the rules of marketing in today's society remains unchanged: *Be careful to keep the followers you have while you seek to add new followers.* It is a no-brainer, really—as we seek to reach more people, we want to do it in a way that does not cause us to lose those we have already won over. It is smart marketing.

But John rejected the idea. Just a few verses after the religious leaders tested John, we read this:

> The next day John was there again with two of his disciples. When he saw Jesus passing by, he said, "Look, the Lamb of God!"
>
> When the two disciples heard him say this, they followed Jesus. (vv. 35–37)

In the blink of an eye, John lost two of his disciples to Jesus as a direct result of placing himself in a subservient posture to the King. These were people John had undoubtedly worked hard to draw to his side, and people upon whom John depended. As for any strong leader, John's followers were his greatest assets. But when John saw the King, he proclaimed the King to his people. And when John's followers heard him proclaim the King, they knew enough to immediately leave John and follow the King.

I wonder if we have the humility of John to send people away from us when it is for the purpose of serving the King. I wonder if I even have the vision to see Jesus passing by and doing the work of His Father nearby. Or am I too consumed in the good work that I am doing in my own little area to notice? If I do notice, is my first thought to consider what part of my work might need to die in order to support the work that He is doing? Do my proclamations of the King result in others choosing to follow Him? The answer should be yes. We should always be looking for ways for Him to increase—even if one of those ways means that we must decrease.

Pointing others to the King may cost you some of your people. In the case of John, one of those people was Andrew, who recruited his brother, Peter (John 1:40–42). In order for Jesus to add some of His most important disciples, John had to lose some of his most important disciples. In the same way, if we are not open to losing some of our people, we may be robbing them of their own discovery of the King. We should seek to draw others to our message, absolutely! But we must never lose sight of the fact that the reason for doing so is ultimately to point them onward to their own discovery of the King.

> We should always be looking for ways for Him to increase— even if one of those ways is that we must decrease.

THE BRIDEGROOM'S JOY

John was losing people to Jesus, and he was losing influence to Jesus. In turn, John's disciples were losing their influence and their claim to fame, and they did not like it. Eventually it boiled over to a point that John's disciples approached him and complained, "Rabbi, that man who was with you on the other side of the Jordan—the one you testified about—look, he is baptizing, and everyone is going to him" (John 3:26).

In one sense, it is hard to fault John's disciples. They had devoted their lives to and given up their careers for John's cause. Their ambitions and identities were wrapped up in John. If John diminished, they diminished. So it is difficult to blame them in that regard. But they were missing the entire point of John's ministry—a point that John had been very vocal about: *John was not the Messiah*.

Listen to John's response:

A person can receive only what is given them from heaven. You yourselves can testify that I said, "I am not the Messiah but am sent ahead of him." The bride belongs to the bridegroom. The friend who attends the bridegroom waits and listens for him, and is full of joy when he hears the bridegroom's voice. That joy is mine, and it is now complete. He must become greater; I must become less. (vv. 27–30)

What a beautiful word picture. John acknowledged that he was diminishing in stature and influence as a result of

Jesus. But John's heart was so set on fully discovering the King, and on helping the King fulfill His mission, he did not express one ounce of regret. In fact, he said just the opposite. John's disciples were looking for validation, but John was interested in associating with the Messiah. His joy was rooted in his association with the Messiah. The Messiah's joy was, in fact, his joy.

The King had called John to a specific mission. But to fulfill that mission, John had to do more than pursue the King. John had to lay down his reputation and status in order to fully discover the King.

John recognized that he was not the Bridegroom. But he was most certainly the friend of the Bridegroom, and he reveled in the front-row seat he had been given to observe his Friend coming for His bride. It was a moment of great joy for him, even though it came with a very clear understanding that the Messiah would permanently displace him.

John simply responded, "He must become greater; I must become less."

Do you take joy in being the friend of the Bridegroom?

Is your joy rooted within the joy of the Bridegroom?

Are there areas of your life where you need to decrease in order for the King to increase?

Do not miss the great joy—and discovery—that comes with being a friend of the Bridegroom!

BELIEF IN THE VOID

Some of the King's message to us is difficult to comprehend. Actually, that is an understatement. Everything the King is telling us to do is impossible for us to fully grasp unless the Almighty Himself communicates it to our spirits.

Shortly after the story of John we just covered, we land on a discussion between Jesus and His disciples in John 6. Jesus had just finished a more detailed explanation of who He is and what will be required of those who follow Him. Many of the disciples were disheartened by Jesus's words and claimed that Jesus was calling them to an impossible task: "This is a hard teaching. Who can accept it?" (John 6:60).

Jesus answered with yet another explanation, then concluded by saying, "This is why I told you that no one can come to me unless the Father has enabled them" (v. 65).

Now it was Jesus who lost people: "From this time many of his disciples turned back and no longer followed him" (v. 66).

I urge you to dial in on this point. Many who are pursuing the King will abandon the pursuit because they do not understand all of His ways. In the next chapter, we will unpack why full understanding is not a requirement for obedience. But first we must grasp this foundational principle: our discovery of the King will often occur in a place that is void of understanding. Hebrews 11:1 puts it this way: "Now faith is the substance of things hoped for, the evidence of things not seen" (KJV). You and I must learn to be so desperate for the King that we place obedience and devotion to Him ahead of understanding His ways.

I know this sounds a bit like heresy at first. But it is true, and we know it is true because Jesus tells us as much in John 6. We will not always fully understand His ways until the Father enables us to see His ways, but we are called to believe and obey even in the intervening space between hearing the King's ways and understanding the King's ways.

> Will we require understanding in order to choose obedience?

Of course, we also need to come into a more complete understanding of the King's ways. Psalm 25:4 says, "Show me your ways, LORD, teach me your paths." We need to go deeper into our relationship with Him in order to gain an intimate understanding of His commands. But that is a process. It does not happen overnight. It involves a period of walking alongside Him. During that process, the question we must carefully ponder and accurately answer is this: Will we require understanding in order to choose obedience? Belief and faith are required when the proof has not yet been discovered. Rest assured, the proof of our faith exists, but it is not yet in our possession.

What will we do in the intervening time? How will we

respond when we do not understand? Will we put our trust and confidence in the King and His ways despite our lack of understanding? Or will we choose to make our own understanding paramount and walk away from the King?

I challenge you to consider the possibility that true discovery of the King is possible only if we choose Him on the lacking side of our own understanding. If we choose His ways over our own understanding, then the Father will reveal an understanding of His ways to us. But if we choose instead to let our own understanding lead the way, then discovery of the King will continue to evade us.

Let us choose faith even in the absence of proof or understanding. Let us accept the hard teachings of the King, embrace an all-out commitment to learning His ways, and then ask the Father to grant us greater understanding. It will require the guidance of the Holy Spirit, because our own flesh is no help at all (John 6:63).

DISCOVER YOUR VOICE

John's shift from knowing the King to truly discovering Him occurred as a result of recognizing that he was simply a voice in the wilderness (John 1:23). It occurred as a result of embracing the idea of humble subservience to the King. It occurred because he was not afraid to lose influence in order that the King might gain influence. It occurred because his joy was rooted in the Bridegroom's joy. And all of this was evidenced by the way John the Baptist used his voice.

John's discovery of the King involved a number of ways in which he was diminished. And yet I am left with a longing to obtain a title like John's: "a voice in the wilderness." There is little dispute that John found his voice in a significant way. After all, we are still reading his words and learning from his example nearly two thousand years later. That is the kind of discovery of the King I want to find—a discovery that involves professing the King's name in a fashion that will echo for generations to come. I want to discover my voice, and I challenge you to discover yours as well.

CHAPTER EIGHT

Echoes

*I will perpetuate your memory
through all generations;
therefore the nations will praise you
for ever and ever.*

Psalm 45:17

I mentioned previously that my wife, Brooke, and I recently celebrated our tenth wedding anniversary with a trip to Europe. While we were in Dublin, we stayed in a hotel right across from the Kilmainham Gaol (Jail). I knew nothing about the prison before our visit, but we were fortunate enough to take a tour of the facility on the one hundredth anniversary of one of the most significant events in Irish history, which happened within its walls.

To make a long and very important story short, in April 1916, a group of Irish rebels conducted an armed rebellion known as the Easter Rising. The goal of the Rising was not a new one: an independent Irish state. What was new was the careful planning and execution of a plan large enough to carry with it a bit of movement. Still, after a week of fighting, British troops suppressed the Rising, and many of the rebel leaders were arrested and thrown into Kilmainham Gaol.

The events that unfolded in the days to follow dramatically changed the course of Irish history. Beginning on May 3 and continuing through May 12, fourteen leaders of the Rising were executed at Kilmainham Gaol. May 4, the day we visited the prison, marked the hundred-year anniversary of the day four of those leaders—Joseph Plunkett, William Pearse, Edward Daly, and Michael O'Hanrahan—faced the firing squad. Brooke and I saw their stone cells, walked the drafty passages they were led through on the way to be executed, and then stood on the very spot where they paid the ultimate price for a cause in which they believed. Before the execution of these fourteen leaders of the Rising, Irish public opinion was opposed to the effort to overthrow British rule. After the executions, public opinion turned overwhelmingly in favor of the rebellion. The end result—after many more years of struggle—was the establishment of the Irish state known today as Ireland.

As Brooke and I toured the dark and damp prison, the walls echoed with the tour guide's stories of those who had toiled and died there for a cause greater than their own. Stories of people like Joseph Plunkett and Grace Gifford, who were married in the prison chapel on the evening of May 3, 1916, just hours before Joseph was executed on the morning of May 4.

I was struck by the fact that each of the fourteen executed after the Rising went to his grave with no idea that his actions had made a pivotal difference. At the time of their deaths, the Rising had been quelled, and a majority of their neighbors were content to leave it at that. As far as those who were executed knew, they were dying for a cause that had failed. As I stood on the spot of the executions, I wondered if any of them had any inkling that the echoes of their actions would have such a dramatic impact.

So often, when we begin to walk in true discovery of the King and lend our voice to His cause, it appears that the message falls on deaf ears. It seems as though our words and our actions make no impact at all. But that is before the echoes. Psalm 45:17 says, "I will perpetuate your memory through all generations; therefore the nations will praise you for ever and ever." In other words, the echoes of what we do and say will reverberate loud and clear long after we draw our last breath.

Are we living with those echoes in mind? Because those echoes will reach far more people, and have a far greater impact, than it might seem when we first utter the words or take the actions.

> It seems as though our words and our actions make no impact at all. But that is before the echoes.

The echoes *will* happen, and they *will* have an impact. But will the impact be for the glory of the King? Are we living for something beyond ourselves? Are we choosing a destiny and a legacy that extends beyond this life and into eternity?

One final observation from Kilmainham Gaol. Because it was the hundred-year anniversary, the courtyard where the executions took place—Stonebreaker's Yard—was adorned with commemorative wreaths in honor of those who gave their lives. Most included a note from a surviving family member or loved one. But what struck me most was the wording of the notes written by the Irish government, which read as follows:

In ómós [name] a cuireadh chun báis cothrom an lae seo i 1916 ar son na hÉireann. Rialtas na hÉireann

In honour of [name] who was executed on this day in 1916 for the cause of Ireland. Government of Ireland[1]

For the cause of Ireland. One hundred years after their death, those executed are still remembered for having laid down their lives for a cause greater than themselves—the cause of Ireland.

One hundred years from now, what echoes will our words and actions create? Will they continue to impact those who come after us? Will they trumpet the majesty of the King? Will they ring out for the cause of the King?

Our legacy will be determined by what is contained in the echoes we leave behind. May those echoes ring out with evidence of a life devoted to the King! And may we not be discouraged when our efforts at first appear to be in vain. We are committing to a cause greater than ourselves, and the echoes of our impact will not be contained by the limits of our lifetime.

THE SIN ECHO

When we fully discover the King, our lives will echo positively through the generations to come. But there is a sobering side to this concept of echoes as well. Many of the spiritual struggles we face are ones that have been passed down to us by previous generations. In the same way, the issues we struggle with are likely the ones that our children will grapple with long after we are gone. Exodus 34:7 and Deuteronomy 5:9 describe it as punishing the children and their children for the sin of the parents to the third and fourth generation. I call it the sin echo. Sin has staying power. It has an invasive ability to permeate our souls, infect our lives, and even carry through to our children and their children.

> Our legacy will be determined by what is contained in the echoes we leave behind.

Now, I want to clearly and firmly state that we have victory over sin through Jesus's death on the cross (Colossians 2:15). We lay hold of that victory by confessing our sin, and we are promised complete cleansing of it (1 John 1:9). So this is a message of great victory and not one of condemnation! At the same time, we must be aware of the sin echoes that have been passed on to us as well as those we may be passing on to future generations.

I will attest from personal experience that it takes this

kind of generational focus to overcome many of our challenges. I find it so easy to rationalize "small" sins when I focus only on the impact I can see. I excuse my sin because "it is not hurting anyone." But that rationale ignores the generational sin echo and paves the way for a tolerance of sin in my life.

But when we live mindful of the sin echo, it serves as a significant safeguard for us. None of us wants to saddle our children with our struggles. What tremendous motivation to deal with those things now and stop the sin echo in its tracks!

OBEDIENCE OVER UNDERSTANDING

Discovery of the King often involves laying aside our own understanding. In the Old Testament, Gideon was repeatedly called to tasks that made no sense. Each task made a little less sense than the last and jeopardized Gideon's life a bit more.

First, God called Gideon to save Israel from the Midianites, and Gideon was overwhelmed (Judges 6:14–16). In fact, Gideon was overwhelmed to the point of asking God for a tangible sign that He was serious. On back-to-back nights, God confirmed His instructions through a sheep's fleece that Gideon put out. On the first night, the fleece was wet and the grass dry; on the second night, the grass was wet but the fleece dry (vv. 36–40). This miracle permeates all the way into today's English language with the term *Gideon's fleece*. But the larger point for us is that while God confirmed His instruction to Gideon, He did not remove Gideon's lack of understanding. Gideon still did not understand how he could possibly succeed, but he moved forward in obedience anyway.

Next, Gideon was instructed to follow the tried-and-true battle strategy of using the smallest possible army to defeat the enemy. Of course, by "tried-and-true," I mean that it is the surest way to be soundly defeated. Frankly, it was a dangerous instruction. Listen carefully to what Gideon was told:

> The LORD said to Gideon, "You have too many men. I cannot deliver Midian into their hands, or Israel would boast against me, 'My own strength has saved me.' Now announce to the army, 'Anyone who trembles with fear may turn back and leave Mount Gilead.'" So twenty-two thousand men left, while ten thousand remained. (Judges 7:2–3)

Along with the obvious foolishness that was sending twenty-two thousand of his thirty-two thousand men home just before battle, listen again to the reason God gave to Gideon: "I cannot deliver Midian into their hands, or Israel would boast against me, 'My own strength has saved me.'" Can you imagine being in Gideon's shoes in this moment? You have been given a dangerous assignment that is beyond your ability. You are not even sure why the assignment is yours, but to make matters worse, you have just been told to send most of your army home. To top it off, the reason you are given for sending the men home is that keeping them around might give you the strength necessary to win the victory. You are told the odds are *not long enough* if you keep the men around, so you must send them home in order to make the odds so long you cannot possibly win. Talk about an instruction that required obedience without understanding!

But Gideon obeyed in the absence of understanding.

His reward? The King asked for more foolish obedience.

But the LORD said to Gideon, "There are still too many men. Take them down to the water, and I will thin them out for you there. If I say, 'This one shall go with you,' he shall go; but if I say, 'This one shall not go with you,' he shall not go."

So Gideon took the men down to the water. There the LORD told him, "Separate those who lap the water with their tongues as a dog laps from those who kneel down to drink." Three hundred of them drank from cupped hands, lapping like dogs. All the rest got down on their knees to drink.

The LORD said to Gideon, "With the three hundred men that lapped I will save you and give the Midianites into your hands. Let all the others go home." (vv. 4–7)

The King's instruction to Gideon was to take only three hundred men into battle to defeat the Midianites. Now, while we are not told exactly how many men the Midianites had, we do know they so oppressed Israel that the Israelites were forced to regularly hide in caves (Judges 6:2). We also know that the Midianites routinely pillaged the Israelites' crops and livestock (vv. 3–5), and that "it was impossible to count them or their camels" (v. 5). Oh, and did I mention that the Midianites prepared for this battle by joining forces with the Amalekites and other neighboring armies (v. 33)? It is safe to say Gideon faced long odds even with his original thirty-two thousand men. The task became humanly impossible with ten thousand men, and it was a suicide mission with only three hundred men.

Gideon had every reason to question this final instruction. It did not make sense. It was dangerous. It was plainly foolish. It would make perfect sense to at least question the instruction as he had done previously. Had I been in Gideon's shoes, I would have been looking for more miraculous confirmation at this point. But listen to the simplicity of Gideon's response:

So Gideon sent the rest of the Israelites home but kept the three hundred, who took over the provisions and trumpets of the others. (Judges 7:8)

Gideon simply obeyed. There is no doubt he still lacked any understanding of why he was to follow these dangerous and foolish instructions. But Gideon was fully invested in the idea that the battle would be fought on the King's terms and that he was walking in discovery of the King. Gideon did not understand. In fact, he was extremely frightened. But this time he did not question the instruction. He respected the King's authority, and he obeyed. The King confirmed what He wanted Gideon to do, and Gideon was determined to walk in obedience no matter the merit of the instruction.

COMMIT TO OBEDIENCE

When I reflect on my own life, I do not see much of this type of obedience. I see some obedience in situations where the King's instructions make sense. I even see obedience in times when I had some resistance or opposition but was able to make a rational case for the potential of victory. I see a pattern of weighing the King's instructions against my own ability to carry them out. And I see a decision-making process that conditions obedience on my own understanding. To be candid, that is weak and easy obedience. That is trusting in my own strength. I am severely limiting what the King can do through me, because I am denying Him permission to work beyond my human bounds and frailties. In reality, that is not obedience at all.

Gideon had decided on obedience even in the absence of understanding, but he was still afraid. And who could blame him? He was choosing to act upon the word of the King rather than the circumstances that were around him. The same enemy that had caused twenty-two thousand of his original thirty-two thousand men to go home in fear was still camped within sight. There was plenty of cause to be afraid, and Gideon was.

I love how the King dealt with Gideon's fear. When the time to attack came, He gave Gideon a way to overcome that fear—a way to confirm yet again that the victory would be given to him. The King instructed Gideon in this way:

> Get up, go down against the camp, because I am going to give it into your hands. If you are afraid to attack, go down to the camp with your servant Purah and listen to what they are saying. Afterward, you will be encouraged to attack the camp. (vv. 9–11)

The King wants our all-out obedience. In order to obtain it, He will sometimes call us into dangerous and fearful situations. He does this for two reasons: first, to accomplish big things through us, and second, to provide us with an opportunity to demonstrate our obedience at any cost. But make no mistake about it—the King is after our obedience, not our fear. In fact, when we are moving forward in His strength, He would have us to be "bold as a lion" (Proverbs 28:1), not moving forward timidly, crippled with fear. So do not be surprised if, once He has secured your obedience, He demonstrates that He has in fact gone before you. Read what Gideon and his servant heard when they went down to the Midianite camp:

> Gideon arrived just as a man was telling a friend his dream. "I had a dream," he was saying. "A round loaf of barley bread came tumbling into the Midianite camp. It struck the tent with such force that the tent overturned and collapsed."
>
> His friend responded, "This can be nothing other than the sword of Gideon son of Joash, the Israelite. God has given the Midianites and the whole camp into his hands."
>
> When Gideon heard the dream and its interpretation, he bowed down and worshiped. He returned to the camp of Israel and called out, "Get up! The LORD has given the Midianite camp into your hands." (vv. 13–15)

The King had already delivered the Midianites into Gideon's hands. The most astonishing part is that *even the Midianites knew it in advance*! While Gideon was still dealing with fear because of the overwhelming odds against him, the King was using fear to paralyze the enemy! In reality, Israel had already won the victory, because when Gideon and his three hundred men did finally move in against the Midianite camp, they did not even have to raise their weapons. Gideon and his men simply blew their trumpets, smashed their jars, and shouted this declaration: "A sword for the LORD and for Gideon!" (v. 20). Upon hearing these sounds, the Midianites turned on each other and then fled. The impossible victory was achieved without lifting a single weapon.

Gideon's obedience never hinged on his own understanding.

Even when he finally attained an assurance that the King was in control, Gideon never understood why he was being asked to obey in this foolish way. But it is refreshing to me that the King is perfectly comfortable engaging Gideon's repeated and honest candor. Gideon is not afraid to tell the King of his doubts. He makes it clear that he will obey, but he is also candid about his misgivings.

The King wants our obedience even in the absence of understanding. But that does not mean He wants us to obey without conversing with Him. In fact, the King craves an honest dialogue with us. One of the very reasons He calls us into challenges that are beyond us is to trigger our dialogue with Him. The King does not want to be found at the end of our pursuit. He wants a relationship with us as we walk along our life's journey. The King isn't after the result of obedience as much as He is after the discovery of Him that occurs as we interact with Him toward that result. He wants to be discovered, and part of that discovery is an honest dialogue about our fears. He gives us permission to bring our doubts to Him honestly.

> The King craves an honest dialogue with us.

But in the end, whether the fear is removed or it remains, *understanding is not a prerequisite for obedience.* Let us together choose obedience in advance and commit to that obedience even when we do not understand. Let us keep in mind the generational echoes of our lives and dedicate ourselves to a cause greater than ourselves—the cause of the King.

CHAPTER NINE
Walk in the King's Power

*Finally, be strong in the Lord
and in his mighty power.*

Ephesians 6:10

There may be no grittier depiction of discovering the King than that of King David. David was himself pursued by God to be made king (1 Samuel 16). He knew the mighty hand of the King, and as a result he knew victories that included slaying a lion and a bear (1 Samuel 17:34–35), killing a giant (1 Samuel 17), repeatedly escaping the wrath of a king who wanted to kill him (1 Samuel 19–26), and eventually assuming the throne of that king (2 Samuel 5:3). In short, David was not a man who was unaware of the awesome power of the King. To the contrary, the King's power had been clearly evident in David's life from a very young age. David lived his entire life operating within that power. He not only witnessed it firsthand, but he knew the reality of possessing that power within his own being. He was a conductor of the King's power.

And then David fell.

My natural tendency is to believe that once we discover and experience the awesome power of the King in an intimate way, we will easily resist the temptations of the world for the rest of our lives. That is simply not true. In fact, once we know the power of the King firsthand, we become a greater threat to the enemy and more worthy of his targeting. Ephesians 6 encourages us to "be strong in the Lord and in his mighty power," but it also assures us that we will have to do so in the face of "spiritual forces of evil in the heavenly realms" (vv. 10–12). Simply put, a deeper discovery of the King will increase the frequency and intensity of the attacks on us. As we grow closer to the King and begin to walk in more of His power, we will climb the enemy's hit list.

In the case of David, lust was the enemy's weapon of choice. Lust proved to be not only the easiest way to wound David but also a sin that would compound itself again and again in David's life. In 2 Samuel 11, David saw Bathsheba and he lusted. Then he acted on that lust. Then he tried to cover up that lust. When his cover-up failed, he conspired to have Bathsheba's husband killed in cold blood. His conspiracy cost many others their lives as well, and it caused his nation to suffer an unnecessary military defeat. After all this, David was still caught in the grip of his lust, and he still took Bathsheba as his own. Simply put, King David knew the power of the King better than anyone, but he still fell in a dramatic and overwhelmingly significant way.

But that is, of course, not the end of the story. The lineage of David and Bathsheba would lead directly to Jesus. Joseph, the earthly father of Jesus, was a descendant of David and Bathsheba (Matthew 1:1–17). Many biblical historians believe that Mary, the virgin mother of Jesus, was also a descendant of David according to Luke 3:23–38. This story of redemption should give us great hope when we have failed miserably.

However, as we discuss how to discover the King by asking questions at life's crossroads, I want to zero in on how we should respond in those moments that come just after a monumental event—be it a significant victory or a significant setback. How do we leverage those pivotal moments to propel us forward in our walk with the King rather than allow them to trap us in reliving what has already occurred?

MOVING FROM SINNER
TO CONQUERING SINNER

In the spring and summer of 2015, I experienced a time of great discovery of, and walking with, the King. It was a season of great intimacy with my Savior and a period of renewed intensity and personal revelation through both my private devotional time and my public life. I felt closer to the King than I had in several years, and I saw abundant evidence of that intimate relationship in my life. It was also a time in which God dealt with some areas of my heart that needed a course correction—areas in which the selfish desires of my heart had been permitted to lead rather than be subservient to the King's desires for my life. The result was a tremendous exuberance as each day brought more invigorating interaction and dialogue with the King.

My expectation was that the positive forward momentum in my walk with the King would leave me almost worry-free—or at least with reduced conflict. After all, while some of the progress was dealing with trouble areas in my heart, all of it was drawing me closer to the King and deeper into the center of His will for my life. But then I discovered something that was difficult for me to accept. I discovered additional areas of my heart that needed work. I discovered new aspects of myself that were out of step with the King. The honest truth is that the discovery depressed me. The revelation of additional areas that needed to be addressed left me feeling defeated. I had been encouraged by "my" progress and had taken on an expectation that the dirty work was over and that it was now time to move on into the more pleasant aspects of my walk with the King. I am sure it is patently obvious that I was missing the point. If I wanted a deeper relationship with the King, I would need to continue dealing with the shortcomings of my human heart.

The bottom line is that my spirit felt heavy because I was focused on the things God was revealing that I had yet to learn. I had to learn how to deal with the fact that my growing relationship with the King is never a finished work. As we grow toward the King, there will *always* be new areas of darkness in our hearts to address. This should not be a debilitating fact, as it was for me for a time. In fact, we should grow significantly in confidence as we take strides in conquering sin. That confidence should then be used to address the new areas of sin we discover. It is lethal if we assume our past conquering is enough. There will certainly be a need for more conquering, as the enemy will not simply cede the fight. But it is equally lethal if we are defeated by the realization that there are new areas of our hearts to address.

We will never achieve a full likeness of Christ here on earth. To pretend otherwise is extremely dangerous. Our focus needs to be on how far God has brought us. That will in turn give us confidence to address those new problematic areas that are revealed to us. If we are content with what God has done in our past, then we open ourselves up to a Bathsheba moment.

> It is lethal if we assume our past conquering is enough.

We should mark the past and celebrate it, absolutely. But we must also use the past—and the conquering that occurred there—to address the new challenges and the new refining the King has for us. We must take our eyes off the past and focus them forward. That is what moves us from *sinners* to *conquering sinners*.

And when we fall—as David fell—we must find the humility to face those failures head-on. In doing so, we will find the strength to break free of their bonds and refuse to be defined by our failures. The King had great plans for King David on the other side of his failure. But those plans could not be achieved until King David fully dealt with his sin and again set his eyes forward. King David fell, but he would rise again as a result of setting his eyes not on his failures but on the King.

SAND FILTERS

After our youngest daughter, Hope, was born, we moved a little farther from the city in order to get a "real" house. For the most part, a "real" house meant exactly one thing to us: no shared walls with neighbors. Sure, there were other characteristics that we had in mind—things like a nice-size yard for the kids, an extra bedroom for guests, and a quiet street. But those things were all icing on the cake, so to speak. After experiencing three newborns in a townhome that shared walls on three sides with neighbors, we mainly wanted a home that wasn't attached to anyone else's. We wanted to no longer have our babies awakened in the middle of the night because of the party happening next door. We didn't want to have to worry about keeping our neighbors awake because one of our babies was crying. We just needed a bit of separation from the rest of the world.

Our wish list was simple. So it was somewhat surprising that we ended up getting a house with a pool. It was an old pool in need of some repair and TLC, but it was a pool nonetheless. In the years that would follow, we would see God's hand at work in moving us to a house with a pool, because it quickly became a place of peace for Jude. Jude is kind, considerate, and sharp as a tack. But as I shared previously, Jude also has to work harder than most to develop some of his basic skills. It is a source of nearly constant frustration for him.

But there is no frustration for Jude in the pool. He is at complete peace in the water, especially as he swims underneath the surface. Something about the stillness and the pressure of being underwater speaks to Jude, and he will spend long amounts of time doing nothing but swimming beneath the water between brief gulps of air at the surface. He will jump off the diving board for extra momentum in order to sit at the bottom of the pool in the deep end before swimming back to the top to do it all over again.

The bottom line is we needed the pool even though we did not realize it.

One of the ramifications of having the pool, however, is that I have had to learn how to care for a pool. As those of you who have a pool can attest, it is not overly difficult, but it does take consistent attention. The chemical balance of the water must be regularly monitored and the proper levels of several components maintained. Our pool filtering equipment needs updating, but until that happens, it is operating with only one intake from the pool. This presents an additional challenge, because moving the water through the bed of sand that resides inside the filter is by far the most important part of keeping the pool clean. To quote the owner of the local pool store, keeping a pool clean is "10 percent chemical and 90 percent filtration." That from a guy who makes his living selling pool chemicals!

So often it is the same with us. We spend all of our time looking at the dirt in our lives and trying to come up with the correct "chemical" solution to clean it up. We want a magical mix of theology, knowledge, and inspiration to make it all go away. But theology, knowledge, and inspiration are worthless if we do not also submit to the refining process that separates the clean from the unclean in our hearts. It is not always fun to be pressed through a filter for the purpose of purification, but it is absolutely necessary if we are to truly experience cleansing.

We know from Scripture that refining happens through knowing the Word of the King (Psalm 119:11) and occurs because of the sacrifice Jesus made on the cross. But I all too often forget that it also happens through close, honest relationships with others who will faithfully apply God's Word to my life. Proverbs 27:17 puts it this way: "As iron sharpens iron, so one person sharpens another."

We desperately need the filter of other believers in our lives in order to remove the muck and the filth from our hearts. It can be very unnatural for me to seek out this kind of input in my life, but I desperately need it. After all, purification is 90 percent filtration. Filtration requires putting my life though the cleansing fire of God's Word and the sharpening process that is relationship with others. Let us not forfeit the benefits of being forced through the sand filters in our lives.

RISING AGAIN

To close this discussion about keeping our eyes forward in order to move past a failure, I want to return to King David. To move past his failure, King David had to confront it. But I propose that the foundation for King David's ability to confront his failure and to move forward into discovering and walking with the King was laid well *before* he fell.

Second Samuel 5:3 says, "When all the elders of Israel had come to King David at Hebron, the king made a covenant with them at Hebron before the LORD, and they anointed David king over Israel."

When David became Israel's king, he made a covenant with God and the people. We are not given the exact terms of the covenant, but we can be sure that taking another man's wife and having that man killed to cover the crime had to be a severe violation of the covenant. In order to rise again, David would need to return to this covenant. Here lies the value of laying down markers and covenants with those we love and trust. When we sin, our judgment gets clouded. But if we set out in advance the terms by which we are promising to live, we can return to them in times of failure. The covenant becomes an anchor for our souls.

Had David decided this sin was too big to overcome, his life and legacy would have been defined by that sin. But the King does not define us by our failures. Instead, He calls us to victory on the other side of them. He calls us to return to our original covenant and into a deeper and more meaningful walk with Him.

Our ability to walk into that call is greatly enhanced if we, like David, have a previously established covenant to which we can return. Have you made a covenant with the King? Have you not only accepted the saving grace of the King but also dedicated your time and abilities to Him? If we have made the covenant in advance, then it will serve as a lighthouse on the shore if we find ourselves in a place of failure. It will serve as a place to which we can return.

It is again helpful to consider what the King sees when He looks on us. What does the King see when His eyes fall on our sin-stained souls? David should have been grateful if the King simply looked upon him with mercy rather than wrath. But he received so much more than that. Even after all of the scheming and lusting and killing, when the King looked at David, He still saw the man he was called to be once he returned to a covenant relationship with the King. The King did not see the man David was but rather the man he would be on the other side of his sin. Even in the midst of David's shocking sin, the King saw a man after His own heart (Acts 13:22).

REPENTANCE IS DISCOVERY

David's covenant with the King provided a solid foundation to which David could return and rebuild his life. But turning from his sin and returning to that foundation came at a price. It also required contrition and humility. It required a realignment of David's own view of himself.

When the prophet Nathan boldly confronted David about his sin, the path to David's restoration began with his admission, "I have sinned against the LORD" (2 Samuel 12:13). But it is the immediacy of David's restoration that impacts me. In the moment after David uttered those words, Nathan responded, "The LORD has taken away your sin" (v. 13). There were still heavy consequences for David to face (his son conceived with Bathsheba would die despite David's

> The King does not define us by our failures. Instead, He calls us to victory on the other side of them.

pleading with God to save him [2 Samuel 12:14–18]), but when David voiced a turning away from his sin, the King welcomed him back into a covenant relationship.

As we begin to transition into how we can lead lives centered on service to the King, we must consider David's example. What did David do to accomplish his return to the King?

He knelt and confessed.

David was able to successfully turn his eyes forward

to that which was still ahead. In fact, his most important legacy was still ahead of him, as it was through Bathsheba that King Solomon was born and through the descendants of King Solomon that the King of kings would enter the world. David had plenty of reasons to once again turn his eyes forward. But to take his eyes off of what he was leaving behind, he had to kneel in genuine repentance before the King.

It is no different for us. The King has already paid the ultimate price for us. But if we are to discover the King, we must first respond by kneeling before Him. We have all fallen (Romans 3:23), and each of us will fall again. Will we be defeated by that sin, or will we—like David—kneel in repentance? Will we humbly submit to a refining process that separates out the unclean in our hearts? Will we establish a covenant with the King and return to it in times of failure?

> If we are to discover the King, we must first respond by kneeling before Him.

Sin is real, and we are all prone to its lure. But sin has absolutely no power over those who will kneel in repentance. Those who kneel will be found as more than conquerors (Romans 8:37). Those who kneel will move from sinners to saints who have conquered sin!

CHAPTER TEN
Surrender

At the name of Jesus every knee should bow,
in heaven and on earth and under the earth.

Philippians 2:10

Why must I endure this struggle?"

It sounds like a question from our own lives. It is a plea that seems as if it should be reserved for the weak and dependent. It is a petition suitable for a peasant and is certainly not something you would expect to hear from the lips of a king, much less *the* King.

And yet this is what the King Himself asked of His Father as the hour of His crucifixion drew near. Each of the first three Gospels contains a gripping account of Jesus's physical and spiritual struggle to find the courage necessary to face His own death.[1] This struggle took place in the Garden of Gethsemane, as Jesus prayed to His Father one last time before being betrayed. Jesus knew full well that His mission was to conquer sin and death by taking the sin of others onto Himself. He knew that the mission required His own death. He was committed to fulfilling that mission. And yet He was struggling with the gravity of it all. I think it is fair to say that the fully human part of Jesus was afraid to face the pain and suffering that was just around the corner.

Each of these Gospel accounts contains a nearly identical plea from Jesus to the Father: "If it is possible, may this cup be taken from me. Yet not as I will, but as you will" (Matthew 26:39). In fact, in Matthew's account, Jesus makes this plea twice. Between the two pleas He finds His disciples too weak to pray with Him in His hour of greatest need:

> Going a little farther, he fell with his face to the ground and prayed, "My Father, if it is possible, may this cup be taken from me. Yet not as I will, but as you will."
>
> Then he returned to his disciples and found them sleeping. "Couldn't you men keep watch with me for one hour?" he asked Peter. "Watch and pray so that you will not fall into temptation. The spirit is willing, but the flesh is weak."
>
> He went away a second time and prayed, "My Father, if it is not possible for this cup to be taken away unless I drink it, may your will be done." (vv. 39–42)

There can be no two ways about it—Jesus was desperate to escape what was coming. He was afraid of what was coming. Almost more than anything, He wanted a way out.

We can relate to Jesus in this moment. While we have never been called to take on the sin of the world, and most who read these words will never face their own crucifixion (though a growing number of Christians in our world today face exactly that), we face our own difficulties that we are desperate to have taken from us. We face challenges and opposition that we would give nearly anything to escape. We may even ask, as Jesus did, that "this cup be taken from me." It is a fair petition for us to make.

But when I look at my own life, I am curious to find how often my petition stops there. I am left wondering why I do not model the second part of Jesus's plea—the part where He relinquishes control to the Father. The part where He surrenders His will to the Father's. The part where He kneels physically and figuratively before the altar in surrender.

Here are His words again: "Yet not as I will, but as you will" (v. 39).

And again after a second plea for the cup to be taken from Him: "My Father, if it is not possible for this cup to be taken away unless I drink it, may your will be done" (v. 42).

Jesus is afraid. He is desperate for another way to complete the mission. *But He is even more desperate for the will of His Father.* His heart is set on fulfilling what His Father has called Him to do, and even in His moment of greatest fear and anxiety, He is determined to kneel in surrender to that mission. Jesus begs for another way, but He does not consider abandoning the mission. He does not contemplate a refusal to give of Himself. It is a complete surrender to the Father's will.

The deepest desire of my heart is to live a life of service

to the Father. I tell you honestly that it is a constant struggle for my human heart that is set on so many other things, and I fall short of this mark every single day. But if you and I are going to truly know the King, it is going to require our surrender. If you and I are going to turn our pursuit of the King into a discovery of the King, we must first kneel before Him and surrender our wills. If we are going to fulfill the Father's call on our lives—a call that centers on service in the King's court—we must follow our plea of, "Take this cup from me," with the words of surrender: "Not as I will, but as You will."

WAIT LONG

"Posture is paramount." I distinctly remember hearing those three words as a seven-year-old sitting in our neighbors' basement alongside my sister and several other children for a penmanship class. We were there to learn cursive writing (not exactly a young boy's idea of a good time on a warm summer morning), and I doubt I really even understood the meaning of *paramount.* I also could not understand what sitting up straight had to do with writing loopy letters that connected to one another. But I knew that "posture is paramount" was Mrs. Ackerman's way of telling me to quit slouching. Further, I was convinced that Mrs. Ackerman wanted me to sit up straight for reasons other than the impact it would have on my writing.

Looking back on it, I am even more convinced of it.

Our posture in life impacts everything. The way in which I position my heart, mind, and body plays a huge role in determining how I will respond to both victory and adversity in my life. So often, my ability to respond in a way that creates discovery of the King depends most on the posture of my life leading into that event. An opportunity for service to the King is best recognized and seized upon if the posture of my heart is prepared in advance for that opportunity.

In Gethsemane, as Jesus grappled in prayer with His Father asking if the cup could be taken from Him, there was another struggle taking place. It was the disciples' struggle to stay awake and in prayer for their Master. It was a struggle to maintain a physical and spiritual posture of covering for Jesus. Before walking deeper into the garden to pray, Jesus had asked them, "Sit here while I go over there and pray" (Matthew 26:36). Peter, James, and John received a bit more detail from Jesus a few moments later: "My soul is overwhelmed with sorrow to the point of death. Stay here and keep watch with me" (v. 38).

> If you and I are going to truly know the King, it is going to require our surrender.

Jesus was preparing to go to His own violent death, and He was afraid. He asked for those closest to Him to settle into a posture of prayer on His behalf and "keep watch with me." In one sense, it seems as if Jesus simply wanted reassurance that He was not alone. In this regard, it must have been devastating to return from grappling in prayer only to find His closest friends sleeping. In fact, *three times* Jesus returned to the disciples, and each time they had given in to the posture of sleep (vv. 36–46). Three times they had failed to provide Jesus with the support and companionship He craved in His hour of need. In that moment, Jesus felt very alone.

I am convinced that Jesus's instruction to the disciples was about more than just His need for support during that dark hour as He faced death. It is clear to me that Jesus was also trying to communicate to His disciples the idea that "posture is paramount." He knew that He was about to leave them and they would need to learn how to assume His mantle of leadership. He was trying to convey to them the principle of *waiting long*. He was giving them a living example of the instruction from Psalm 27:14: "Wait for the LORD; be strong and take heart and wait for the LORD."

Too often we view this waiting as nothing more than stillness. To be sure, there is a quieting component to waiting. I like the way Jesus said it in John 14:27: "Peace I leave with you; my peace I give you. . . . Do not let your hearts be troubled and do not be afraid."

Stillness has a way of settling our hearts and rooting them in the security of the Almighty. But true waiting is not simply sitting by until whatever is to be comes our way. No, waiting on the King involves posturing our lives and our hearts in alignment with His. As we wait on the King, we should be grappling with the things that burden His heart and allowing our hearts to be transformed a bit more toward His. In a time like this, when the disciples were witnessing a heavy heart within the King, they should have assumed a posture of shared struggle and joined their King in facing what was at hand.

Robert Pierce famously wrote, "Let my heart be broken with the things that break the heart of God."[2] There are plenty of times when the posture of the King is not grief or struggle, but rather joy and victory. Yet Pierce skillfully identifies the goal here—we are to be waiting on the King in such a way that our hearts are actually changed to be more like His. When we wait on Him in a way that involves active engagement in the things that move His heart, our hearts are moved by them as well. As a result, we discover the King.

Sometimes the waiting feels long. Sometimes it does not just *feel* long; it *is* long! Often we are tempted to let spiritual sleep win out . . . to rest awhile until the King returns. But the King is returning in search of those who are searching for Him while they wait. He is looking for those who have taken up a posture of preparation. He is seeking those who have chosen an active pursuit of Him over those who have given in to sleep. He is looking for those who have waited long in anticipation of His return.

May we wait long. Our reward will be the fullest discovery of the King.

THE FIRST TO KNEEL

We will all kneel. This fact is foretold in Scripture several times.[3] On Judgment Day, when we all stand to give an account for the way we spent our lives, there will be a distinction in the judgments rendered. We have already covered the Matthew 25 depiction of the sheep being separated from the goats. Those who know the King will enter into eternity with Him, but those who continue to reject Him will be themselves rejected.

> Will we surrender all that we are and all that we have for one goal—to discover and serve the King?

So the judgments on that day will not be equal, but the posture of those receiving the judgments will all be the same. On that day, the glory of the King will be so evident that every person—child of the King or otherwise—will bend his or her knee in submission to the King. And each person will make a final confession of the one true King.

In the end, all will kneel.

But my question for you is, when will you kneel?

Will you and I wait until the end to kneel? Will we wait until the glory and the power of the King overwhelm us into submission on that final day? Or will we be among the first to kneel and to voluntarily go beyond simply professing a belief in the King? Will we surrender all that we are and all that we have for one goal—to discover and serve the King?

The King came "to seek and to save the lost" (Luke 19:10). Our eternity with Him is sealed in the moment we believe in Him and profess His covering for our sins. But, my friends, we will not truly discover the King until we kneel in surrender to His service. An intimate knowledge of the King's face eludes us until we recognize that we must discover His true and full identity through a posture of waiting long.

Make no mistake about it—we will all kneel. On that day, none will dispute the power and authority of the King. But let us not be the last to kneel. Let us be the first to kneel! Let it be our deepest desire to experience the full measure of the King's power now, while it can still be used to draw others to Him. We do not have to wait for that day when we stand before the judgment throne. In fact, we *should not* wait until that day. May we choose to kneel now in order to discover Him more fully before our time on earth is done.

If we kneel first, the result will be a life of renewed service to the King. The blessing will be a shared experience with the King and a greater acquisition of the King's heart.

"FEED MY SHEEP"

Feeding and caring for sheep is a dirty and thankless job. It will wear your fingers to the bone, and in return you often get nothing but rudeness from the sheep. They will kick you, spit on you, and bite you.

You see, while sheep are known for recognizing the voice of their shepherd and resting within his care, they also possess a strong stubborn streak and a tendency to bite the hand that feeds them. Shepherding is not a glamorous job, and it is no accident that we have multiple accounts in Scripture (David and Joseph, to name just a couple) where the youngest and lowest-ranking member of the family is given the task of caring for the sheep.

Yet Jesus used the picture of feeding sheep when He gave the apostle Peter this command:

When they had finished eating, Jesus said to Simon Peter, "Simon son of John, do you love me more than these?"

"Yes, Lord," he said, "you know that I love you."

Jesus said, "Feed my lambs."

Again Jesus said, "Simon son of John, do you love me?"

He answered, "Yes, Lord, you know that I love you."

Jesus said, "Take care of my sheep."

The third time he said to him, "Simon son of John, do you love me?"

Peter was hurt because Jesus asked him the third time, "Do you love me?" He said, "Lord, you know all things; you know that I love you."

Jesus said, "Feed my sheep." (John 21:15–17)

If you are already engaged in the task of caring for the King's sheep (His people), you know that Jesus's analogy in John 21 is appropriate. You know that caring for people can be a dirty and thankless job. You know that there are times when the only thing it earns you is the revilement of those you are serving. You know it is probably not a job to be sought out if the goal is a life of ease and luxury.

But feeding sheep is the way we live out our love for the King.

Feeding sheep is what the King has called us to do to demonstrate our love for Him. Not once, not twice, but three times Jesus asks if Peter loves Him. Each time Peter tries to respond yes, but Jesus stops him short and reiterates that He will be convinced of Peter's love when He sees it carried out in the form of service. The timing of this conversation is crucial, as it is after Jesus has been raised from the dead and just before Jesus leaves the disciples and tasks them with being the living embodiment

> Feeding sheep is the way we live out our love for the King.

of His message on earth. Jesus is leaving the disciples with instructions on how to be close to Him once He is gone. He is trying to equip them with an understanding of how to discover Him when His physical presence is not with them. He is trying to impress upon them the importance of service to those around them.

Professing the name of the King is a vital part of knowing Him, but it is not the way we demonstrate our love for Him.

Reciting the King's words will deepen our understanding of His ways, but it is not the way we demonstrate our love for Him.

Telling of the King's mighty works will draw others to Him, but it is not the way we demonstrate our love for Him.

The *demonstration* of love that the King is seeking from us is *our humble service to His sheep.* The King desires that we live our lives in a fashion that places the needs of others above our own. We have every reason to believe that the initial reward for feeding His sheep will be similar to the experience of feeding actual sheep—we will be bitten, kicked, and spit upon.

But, as we will see in part 3, if we are to truly discover the King, we must devote ourselves to caring for His sheep. We must embrace the humility that comes with feeding His sheep. It is the only way to truly discover the King, because the King has concealed Himself in the midst of His sheep.

PART THREE

Serve the King

CHAPTER ELEVEN

Choose Service

Whoever wants to be first must be slave of all.
For even the Son of Man did not come to be served,
but to serve, and to give his life
as a ransom for many.

Mark 10:44–45

I recently had the great honor of standing beside my good friend John as he received his bride, Mary Beth, and they took the vows of marriage. It is always fun to witness two followers of the King pledge their commitment to each other, and that was certainly the case as I watched John and Mary Beth. The setting was a beautiful plantation house in Providence Forge, Virginia, and even an unseasonably hot day could not dampen the joy we all shared with the happy couple.

But it was the unique symbolism of servitude to each other that will linger longest in my mind. Most wedding ceremonies I have been a part of (including my own) have included a midceremony interlude in which the couple demonstrates their commitment to each other through either communion, the lighting of a unity candle, or maybe a shared prayer. This was the first time, however, I have witnessed the bride and groom washing each other's feet. I was struck not only by the appropriate symbolism of service to each other they were vowing, but also by the visual reminder of the service the King modeled for His disciples, and to which each of us is called.

OUR SERVANT KING

In John 13, Jesus and His disciples were participating in the Passover meal and Jesus's death on the cross was drawing near. Jesus, the King, shocked the disciples by demonstrating His love in an extremely humbling fashion:

> [Jesus] took off his outer clothing, and wrapped a towel around his waist. After that, he poured water into a basin and began to wash his disciples' feet, drying them with the towel that was wrapped around him. (vv. 4–5)

Peter was having none of it. He was not going to allow his King to humble Himself in such a dramatic way on his account. Peter exclaimed, "No, you shall never wash my feet" (v. 8). It was a perfectly understandable reaction. Peter had given up all he had because he believed Jesus was the Messiah. Peter was determined to preserve the dignity of his King. He was determined to prevent the humbling of his King—the King he had given everything to serve.

Look at Jesus's response, and Peter's immediate understanding:

> Jesus answered, "Unless I wash you, you have no part with me."

"Then, Lord," Simon Peter replied, "not just my feet but my hands and my head as well!" (vv. 8–9)

Peter wanted all of the King he could get. In his own mind, it was degrading for the King to participate in a foot-washing. But if the cleansing of his feet was a prerequisite for being found in the King, then Peter wanted a full bath! On one hand, we should respond the same way. We should want all of the King. We should want a filling to the point of overflowing, and Peter's expression of this desire is genuine and reflective of a heart fully devoted to the King.

But even in this response, Peter continues to miss the point in one regard. Jesus was modeling His full devotion to the disciples through service and demonstrating what would

> None of us must view ourselves above even the most humbling acts of service to others.

be required for them to fully discover Him. It would require more than simply acknowledging that Jesus was Messiah. A full discovery of the King would have to take the form of service to the King and others. Jesus was demonstrating that none of us must view ourselves above even the most humbling acts of service to others.

Let it not be enough that we search for the King, or even that we find Him and learn to discover Him in new ways.

Let us make it our deepest longing to know Him in a way that we can only experience through service to Him. First Peter 2:9 calls our service to the King a "royal priesthood." So often, the "royal" part is appealing, but the "priesthood" portion is challenging. We want the royal association with the King, but we are not as sure about the sacrificial service that priesthood requires. Like Peter, we attain the appropriate desire for more of the King more readily than we do the call to a lifetime of humility and service.

The idea of a life of service often causes us to recoil. But service is what is required of us, and it is what the King modeled for us. He washed His disciples' feet and gave His life as a ransom for us.[1] Just as my friends John and Mary Beth demonstrated a commitment to service through the symbolism of washing each other's feet, the King demonstrated His commitment to His bride—us—by washing the disciples' feet. He is now calling each of us into a similar life of service. It is not a call for a few, but rather for all who are in the King's court. It is not a call for the weak or the inferior. In fact, it is our highest calling.

WHY SERVE?

If I am honest with you about the state of my heart, the call to service is still an unnatural one for me. I understand intellectually that the King commands me to serve, and I even have a fairly deep well of experience to draw from as confirmation that service is the conduit for discovery. But my heart is still naturally disinclined to choose the seat at the foot of the table, or to allow my eyes to see that Homeless Rodney is really King Rodney. I am far more inclined to notice the worth and merit of myself than I am to assume a subservient posture. I suspect it may always be my natural inclination, and one that requires intentionality to overcome.

But in many regards, that is precisely the point. It is why this call to servitude receives such a high billing in the eternal kingdom—because it requires that we take our eyes off ourselves. It requires a shift in priorities—even if it is a forced shift—away from our own needs and wants, and onto those of others. Once we are focused on the needs of others, we are much more likely to be sensitive to the kingdom opportunities that exist around us.

"THEY ARE JUST LIKE US"

Recently our family attended a baseball game to see the Chicago Cubs play the Washington Nationals. It was, of course, a fantastic evening at the ballpark, even if the Cubs did lose in twelve innings (as any parent can attest, cotton candy more than makes up for any boredom that a four-, five-, and seven-year-old may experience during extra innings). Brooke had to leave early for a church event, but the rest of us stayed until the bitter end—which occurred about five hours after we had arrived at the park.

As we walked back to the parking lot, we passed another family on the side of the road—a family who was begging for money. Our family is trying to be intentional about taking notice of those who find themselves in a position to beg. But even so, I was struck by the vast difference between how I viewed this family and how my children viewed this family.

To be very honest, I saw a professional beggar. I saw a father holding a child as a prop for sympathy. I saw a mother and two older children striking sad poses in order to attract attention from those walking past. I saw the use of emotional facts in the handmade cardboard sign the father was holding: *"I have three kids and they are hungry. Please help."* I saw the father's quick glance through the roll of bills he had already received from those passing by. In short, even though this man was doing something that required far more humility than I possess, my critical heart saw the flaws. My heart saw the portions of the situation that I deemed a touch conniving and the "lucrative" rewards he had already received. I saw the inconsistencies because I was making a snap judgment based on my view of the merits.

But seven-year-old Jude saw none of that. Jude saw only parallels with our family. As we walked past the family, I was hoping the kids had not noticed them. Even though I was trying to be intentional about noticing those in need, I had weighed the merits of this particular situation and found them to be wanting, so I was hoping the kids had been distracted. But Jude tugged on my shirt. He had noticed. And he had noticed much more important things than had I.

"Dad, they have three children, just like us."

"Dad, the three children are hungry."

"Dad, he doesn't have a job to buy food for the children."

"Dad, they don't have a home to sleep in."

"Dad, they are sad."

"Dad, we have to help them."

In the same amount of time it had taken me to make a snap judgment, Jude had made a snap judgment of his own: *"They are just like us."* He had made a snap judgment that we had to help. Jude, in a way that only children seem to be able, had seen our connection to this family without weighing any of the merits.

My heart was simultaneously full at Jude's clarity of vision and grieved at the depravity of my own. Had I learned nothing? The call to service is not altered by the merits (or lack thereof) of those around us. In fact, we are called to give when it is *not* deserved. The call to service has many reasons, but I suggest the first one has nothing to do with the recipient of our efforts, but rather the condition of our own heart. Service has a way of humbling our hearts that nothing else does. It reminds us in a very practical way that it is not about us. It is not even primarily about those we tangibly serve. It is always first and foremost about the King. And the

King has told us to give, "without expecting to get anything back" (Luke 6:35). He has told us to be "servant of all" (Mark 10:44–45 KJV).[2]

Why serve? Because we will never discover the King unless we do.

FREEDOM TO SERVE

Freedom. Liberty. Tranquillity. Each of these is a hallmark of the American pursuit. Truthfully, each is a universal hallmark of the human pursuit, but more readily achieved in some places of the world than others. Every day brings with it fresh reminders of how many of our brothers and sisters around the world live under anything but freedom to serve the King with abandonment. In fact, the application of this book to your life will depend greatly on the lens through which you read it. It will depend on your level of freedom—both literally and spiritually.

For example, if you—like me—are reading this from the relative comfort and freedom of a place that allows you to openly declare the name of the King, your obligation to utilize that freedom is great and extremely practical. On the other hand, if you are among the hundreds of millions around the world living under the restrictive eye of a controlling government, an oppressive power, or even a violent extremist regime, your freedom to live out your service to the King in practical ways will be limited. Your obligation will be to search out opportunities for service within your narrow band of freedom. But, of course, your spiritual obligation to pursue a mind-set of service will be the same.

Galatians 5:13 says, "You, my brothers and sisters, were called to be free. But do not use your freedom to indulge the flesh; rather, serve one another humbly in love." There is both a practical freedom and a spiritual freedom in our call to serve others. It is critical for us to understand both of these, and also to achieve a wide enough perspective to be fully aware of the role we play in the global church and the obligation we have to our brothers and sisters around the world.

On the practical side of the equation, our hearts should be drawn to the plight of the persecuted church around

Why serve? Because we will never discover the King unless we do.

the world. In my line of work, we often use terms like "the church in America," "the church in Syria," or "the African church." These are helpful terms as we consider our obligations to advocate for our brothers and sisters in these regions, but we must be careful to avoid using them in a way that suggests there is more than one church. Of course there are countless expressions of service to the King (in reality, there are as many different expressions as there are individuals pursuing the King). That is one of the most beautiful things about our King—His call to us is unique, and our experience with Him is personal. But we are one church in pursuit of one King,[3] and we have the privilege of using whatever freedom we have on behalf of our brothers and sisters around the world.

We are called to a practical freedom, and I for one am privileged beyond words to be living in a country where I can experience that practical freedom. But am I using that practical freedom to indulge my flesh or in humble service to those around the world who are not free? Am I concerned to the point of action by the billions who are living under all manner of limitations to their freedom—such as the ability to assemble together, the right to freely and publicly express their faith, or even an outright prohibition on confessing the name of the King? Do I use my freedom on their behalf? If I do not, I am not living in true service to the King. If you have a similar practical freedom, true service to the King involves embracing the cause of your persecuted brothers and sisters around the world.

There is an additional practical component to this idea, and it is a sober one. Many of us walk in freedom today, but that freedom may be fleeting. I could point to all manner of geopolitical factors to convince you that religious freedom is waning rather than expanding all around the world. But the geopolitical factors pale in comparison to the promises of persecution we find in Scripture. We are promised that we will be hated because of the King (Mark 13:13), that we are certain to have trouble because of the King (John 16:33), and to expect "fiery trial[s]" because of the King (1 Peter 4:12 KJV).

If you currently live in freedom as I do, rejoice! Use that freedom to advocate for those who are not free! But also live with the sober reality that it may not always be so. Live with the understanding that devotion to the King brings with it a risk of rejection by the world. Live with the expectation of rejection in order to ensure that its possible fruition does not take you by surprise but instead causes you to glorify the King because of it (1 Peter 4:16).

There is great news in all of this! Nothing can separate us from the love of Christ (Romans 8:35). The King has already overcome this world (John 16:33), and if we stand firm in the face of our trials, we will be saved (Matthew 10:22).

> True service to the King involves embracing the cause of your persecuted brothers and sisters around the world.

The end of the story has been written, and the King has already won the victory. Those of us who are members of the global church will not always have the same physical freedoms. But let us use whatever freedoms and liberties we do have in service to the King and on behalf of our persecuted brothers and sisters.

The spiritual component of this freedom to serve is every

bit as real. This is an extraordinarily simple principle, and rather than belabor the point, I challenge you to consider the gravity of this question: Will you choose a life of freedom through service or a life of bondage through indulgence?

The good news is that we can chose freedom. You and I can be free by dedicating ourselves to service.

Practically speaking, if you are free, use that freedom to serve those who are bound. And if you are bound, rejoice in the promise that you are about to overcome!

> You and I can be free by dedicating ourselves to service.

Spiritually speaking, if you desire freedom, pursue service. Service to the King is the key to escaping the bonds of self-centeredness and truly discovering the face of the King.

"Anyone who wants to be first must be the very last, and the servant of all" (Mark 9:35).

"If the Son sets you free, you will be free indeed" (John 8:36).

CHAPTER TWELVE
Fail More

*Do not be afraid. Stand firm
and you will see the deliverance
the LORD will bring you today.*

Exodus 14:13

My first book failed. I shared earlier that it took nearly fifteen years for me to finally step out in obedience to God's call to write. What I did not share is that this is not that first book. We are going to redefine failure in this chapter, but for now it is fair to say my first book failed. At least in the way I typically view failure. After pouring a great amount of time, energy, and passion into the book, committing the results to God, and having the divine blessing of obtaining terrific representation for it, we presented the manuscript to publishers.

I knew very well that most manuscripts do not get published. Actually, that is a dramatic understatement. But I also knew beyond a shadow of a doubt that I was finally walking in obedience to the King. So, while I truly committed the results to God, I assumed His plan included quick publication of the book. I was wrong. Despite a number of interested publishers, the book did not secure a publishing contract. In a word, it failed.

But without that failure, you would not be holding this book. More important, without that failure, I would still be walking in my second decade of direct disobedience. Without that failure, this message of discovery and service to the King would still be unwritten.

I truly believe we need to redefine failure. Failure has a negative connotation, and I believe mistakenly so. Without failure, we often miss out on the place the King is trying to take us on the other side of that failure. Because we fear failure, we are not inclined to step out in service to the King. We would rather avoid failure than take a chance on succeeding through service to the King.

SPACE FOR THE KING

I need to fail more. Looking back on my life to this point, I realize that I have not failed nearly often enough. I say that not as evidence of how great I am, but in fact just the opposite. It is an indictment of how rarely I have stepped outside of my own abilities and into a task where only the King can produce a victory. I have been content to mostly stick to tasks I am convinced I can complete. It is a calculation I make before I agree to start something or to serve somewhere. If my calculation tells me that I have the skills and ability to succeed, I trust in myself and I proceed. But if my calculation tells me that I will fail absent intervention from something or someone, I take a pass and move on to something more within my control.

In doing so, I forfeit the victory the King was planning.

In Exodus 14, the Israelites were finally on their way out

of Egypt after 430 years of slavery. It took ten plagues from God to convince Pharaoh to let the Israelites go, but even then the people were not able to rest in the truth that their deliverance was in God's hands. As soon as Pharaoh started to pursue them, the Israelites said to Moses:

> Was it because there were no graves in Egypt that you brought us to the desert to die? What have you done to us by bringing us out of Egypt? Didn't we say to you in Egypt, "Leave us alone; let us serve the Egyptians"? It would have been better for us to serve the Egyptians than to die in the desert! (vv. 11–12)

The people were terrified to fail. They were terrified of standing back to see what God would do. And who am I to blame them? Clearly, if it was left to their strength and their ability, they were about to be either slaughtered or returned to the captivity and slavery that had been their lot for nearly half a millennium. It was a dire situation, and they were wishing they had not even tried. I can relate. My flesh prefers the status quo over stepping out in faith only to fall on my face. I am so concerned with my reputation that I would rather not step out and see what the King will do. I recognize the King may come through, but what if He does not? It is often a gamble I am not willing to take.

Moses responded to the people, "Do not be afraid. Stand

firm and you will see the deliverance the LORD will bring you today. The Egyptians you see today you will never see again. The LORD will fight for you; you need only to be still" (vv. 13–14).

The message was simple: *This is not about you or your power. This is about what your King will do for you.*

Moses was clearly having his own doubts, because immediately after putting on a brave face for the people, he cried out to God. Moses saw the same thing the people did—they were going to be defeated. He had enough faith to appear confident, but not enough to believe in the deliverance that had been promised. God's response to Moses is blunt and direct: "Why are you crying out to me? Tell the Israelites to move on." My paraphrase is: "I already told you what to do and that I would protect you. Now, quit crying and just do it!"

You see, God wanted to create space in which He could work. He wanted to demonstrate His power in such a way that there would be no disputing who had accomplished the victory. He wanted the Israelites to fail in their escape so that He could succeed in accomplishing it for them!

When I am not willing to step out in faith for things I am unable to accomplish on my own, I am closing the door on the best opportunities for the King to come through for me. If I am not deliberately creating space that I am insufficient to fill, I am limiting the amount of the King's power that can be put on display. If I am only stepping into tasks and ideas that I can handle, the world will see me when those things are accomplished. But when I step into a task that is bigger than me, and when I do so while admitting that it will take the intervention of the King to succeed, the sky is the limit! Or maybe I should say that the Red Sea is not the limit! Because when Moses agreed to walk in God's plan for the Israelites' seemingly futile predicament, the sea could not hold them. The mighty King took control and made a way through the water where there had been no way before.

Moses was afraid of failing. But when God's call to service extended into a place beyond his human ability—and into a place that risked failure—Moses answered the call. Moses chose service to the King even when he was convinced he would fail. Think of the victory that would have been forfeited had Moses chosen not to risk failure!

> This is not about you or your power. This is about what your King will do for you.

Before we move on, let us not miss the numerous miracles that are on display here. The parting of the Red Sea generally demands our attention, and understandably so. But Exodus 14 outlines several miracles working together to provide this escape:

- The angel of God and the pillar of cloud that had been leading the Israelites moved behind them and served as a physical separation from their enemies.
- The Israelites were given light all night long while the Egyptians were cast into darkness, ensuring the two armies would not come together.
- God created confusion—and a chariot malfunction—throughout the Egyptian army, which caused the entire Egyptian army to be in the seabed when God's mighty hand released the waters back in place on top of them.

God performed miracle upon miracle, none of which would have been possible without a willingness to try the impossible. We have to be willing to step into that space.

Our stories may not always be as neatly and quickly redeemed as was the Israelites' crossing of the Red Sea. Sometimes our stepping out in faith into the unknown may not produce a miracle (at least that we can see). Sometimes it will feel like a failure. But we can rest in the confidence of a King who sees in full while we see only in part (1 Corinthians 13:12).

We need to have such a dependent trust in the King that we are willing to fail for Him. We need to understand that He is the omniscient, all-knowing One, and we are not. We need to be willing to step out in service to Him even with the understanding that it may not always end in roaring success. Why? Because that creates space for the King to go to work. He is perfectly capable of accomplishing the work through a mighty miracle. Or He may have a plan that is accomplished through our human failure. Either way, we have to step out.

> We are called to proclaim the good news into every situation and circumstance.

So I challenge you to join me in failing more. I am confident that it will multiply the number of miracles we experience in our lives. It will likely also increase those times where we do not understand what the King is doing. But that is a good thing, because we will have given the King room to work, and the "failure" will serve as evidence that we are operating in an obedience that extends beyond our own human capacity. It will be proof that we are discovering the King!

A BIGGER PLATFORM

Scary is good. Being intimidated and uncomfortable about a task to which we are assigned is exhilarating. It may not be fun in every moment, but it is proof that we are setting our hands to something that is beyond ourselves. If we are never nervous or apprehensive about what lies ahead, we are too comfortable. We are treading a path that is not nearly ambitious enough for the Kingdom. We are playing it far too safe.

The only way to reach more for the King is to step onto the bigger platform that is ahead of you. Scary is good.

At the same time, there will always be a bigger and better platform from which to proclaim the good news. Always. So often this has prevented me from proclaiming the gospel from the platform on which I am currently standing. I justify myself with the idea that I will be more effective if I wait until I am on that bigger and better platform.

There are, of course, multiple fatal flaws with this approach. First, if we are always looking for that time when we have a better platform, we will never actually step out and proclaim. As a result, the strength of our voices will never grow, and when we reach that bigger and better platform, our voices will not be ready. Second, once we do step onto that grand stage and we can see off into the distance, guess what will come into view? An even bigger and better platform. There will always be the temptation to wait for an even grander stage from which to speak. But we are called to proclaim the good news into every situation and circumstance. If we are not willing to do so, our vocal cords will atrophy and those we are walking alongside now will pass by without hearing the good news.

Do not wait for the grander stage. Do not let fear stand in the way. Scary is good. Stand on the platform that is available to you *now*—whether onstage before a crowd or across the table from a neighbor—and boldly proclaim what the

King has done for you. Then do the same from whichever stage—be it large or small—you find yourself on tomorrow.

THREE KEY QUESTIONS

Over the last several years as I have grappled with how to better serve the King, one of the most difficult (and recurring) challenges I have had is reconciling what feels like conflicting commands in Scripture when it comes to searching out new territory from which to proclaim the King.

For example, the righteous are described to be as "bold as a lion" (Proverbs 28:1) and commanded to "go and make disciples of all nations" (Matthew 28:19). Those verses and many others compel me to press forward into as many situations and venues, and to expand the kingdom to as many people, as possible.

But then we read the parable of the feast, in which Jesus says, "When someone invites you to a wedding feast, do not take the place of honor. . . . But when you are invited, take the lowest place" (Luke 14:8–10). The person seated at the lowest place has no speaking role at the feast. That person has no platform from which to communicate to the attendees. Now, the parable goes on to talk about the person being invited forward to a better seat, but I am still left a bit confused about when we are to search out new territory and a broader influence, and when we are to humble ourselves and wait to be called forward.

I am coming to learn that the answer depends largely on three additional questions.

"Is the King Here?"

The first and foundational question is, "Is the King here?"

We should not be rushing ahead of the King but instead leaning on His instruction and guidance. When we are contemplating whether (or how) to step into a new space, we must first confirm whether the King is in that space. We must make sure that it is His mission we are stepping into rather than our own. This is what enables us to be bold as a lion, because we will have already confirmed that the King of kings has prepared the way for us and we are stepping into an assignment He is already in. He is waiting to meet us there and to chart our way forward.

So first ask, "Is the King here?" If the King is in the territory you will be moving into, then ask, "Who will fill the void?"

"Who Will Fill the Void?"

Taking on a new task for the King often leaves a void in the space we are vacating. Who will fill that void? Has the King prepared a way for those in that space to be cared for, or will you be leaving a void for the enemy to fill?

I love Psalm 139:5, which says, "You hem me in behind and before." In other words, if we are walking with the King,

He has not only prepared a way forward in which we should walk, but He has also hemmed us in from behind with protection and someone to care for the ground that we will be vacating.

When you feel called to a new area of service that will require stepping out of something currently entrusted to you, I encourage you to ask the King for confirmation. Ask Him to call someone who can take up the tasks you will be leaving behind. If the King has not yet made provision for that which He has previously entrusted to you, you may need to reconsider whether He is truly calling you to lay it down in favor of a new mission.

"If I Diminish, Will the King Increase?"

The third question is, "If I diminish, will the King increase?"

I have come to expect at least one challenge every day in which "He must become greater; I must become less" (John 3:30). Are there places in your life where you could create space for the King by taking less space for yourself?

In my experience, this often comes in the form of the words I speak. I tend to speak from a me-first perspective. I am learning (slowly) to create a void for the King to fill simply by shifting the focus of my words off of me. We are so wired to create as much space as we can for ourselves—to defend our own turf! But so often, it is not the best way to create room for the King.

This is a redefinition of success—one that we might have previously called failure! Sometimes more territory is the goal, and in those cases, we should proceed with boldness and authority! But sometimes advancing the kingdom means creating a void. It means searching out ways in which we can be diminished in order for Him to increase. We must be willing to say, "He must become greater; I must become less."

Join me in committing to lay aside a fear of failure. Join me in risking failure—and even actually failing—more. Join me in pursuing a commitment to service of the King that is so resolute we are willing to step into the Red Sea. Join me in deliberately seeking out ways to create space for the King by diminishing the space we occupy. Join me in proclaiming the King from both our current platform and any future platform. And when the opportunity to serve—and possibly fail—presents itself, ask yourself three questions:

"Is the King here?"

"Who will fill the void?"

"If I diminish, will the King increase?"

CHAPTER THIRTEEN
Dare the King

LORD, the God of Abraham, Isaac and Israel,
let it be known today that you are God in Israel
and that I am your servant and have done all these things
at your command. Answer me, LORD, answer me,
so these people will know that you, LORD, are God,
and that you are turning their hearts back again.

Elijah's prayer in 1 Kings 18:36–37,

publicly daring the King to show His power

We live timidly. We live shockingly timidly, given that we are servants of the Most High King.

Consider what we have established in these pages so far—Jesus is King over the universe by virtue of His heritage, birth, death, and resurrection, and He is now reigning as the Eternal King. He has personally called each of us into a discovery of, and a service to, Him. He has given us—His servants—access to His power and promised to bind or loose things of both heaven and earth on our behalf (Matthew 16:19; 18:18). While we know we will face persecution in this world (John 16:33), we are promised the King has overcome the world and has secured for us an eternity with Him (John 3:16; 1 John 2:25). Therefore, we have no reason to fear and ought to be the boldest people on the face of the planet.

Yet so often we instead shrink back in either fear or timidity. We mistake service to the King for quiet timidity and mistake His instruction to model meekness for one of weakness. We decline to walk in His power because it is easier to blend in and play it safe. We either doubt that His power is real or we are afraid to walk in it. There are times we decline to walk in it because we are afraid He will not deliver. There are other times we decline to walk in it because we are afraid He *will* deliver.

No more. It is time to walk in the power of the King. It is time to truly desire that His power be on display. And it is time to risk our own reputations by publicly challenging the King to show His power. In short, it is time to dare the King.

A HOLY BOLDNESS

Many of my favorite leaders and visionaries possess a confidence that at times causes them to be labeled as too brash. Certainly there is a balance to strike, but it comforts me a great deal when I see a little holy boldness in leaders I respect. So often, the idea of what it means to be a Christian conjures up images of quiet, pious figures. After all, we are called to be peacemakers and to live for the benefit of others (Matthew 5:9). But where did we get the idea that following the King meant living timidly? When did we decide that service to the King meant shrinking back into the shadows? It certainly did not come from Scripture, because time after time, the great heroes of faith were regular people with regular fears who made a decision to walk in boldness and challenge the culture—or maybe even challenge the King.

The prophet Elijah did more than challenge the King. Elijah dared the King. Elijah set the stage for a miracle— a grandiose stage with an enormous amount of publicity and fanfare, and his own reputation was very much on the line. Elijah decided that he would put it all on the line in service to the King and let the King decide how to end the story. If the King's power did not show up, it was not going to be a result of Elijah's failure to invite Him to be present. It was not going to be because Elijah was afraid to lay it all on the line.

The story is found in 1 Kings 18, and the backdrop was a severe famine brought on by a deep drought that lasted several years. To make matters worse, the famine and the drought occurred as the result of Elijah's own words. The cause of the drought and famine was the sin of King Ahab and the people's worship of the idol god, Baal. But the proclamation of the drought came from the lips of Elijah, and as a result he had been living on the run. King Ahab had been desperately searching for Elijah, and God's prophets were hiding in caves to escape the king's wrath. To put it simply, the country was in deep turmoil, and Elijah was the obvious one to blame.

> Where did we get the idea that following the King meant living timidly?

Sometime during the third year of the famine, God told Elijah to return to Ahab and deliver the news that He would send rain. The fact that Elijah obeyed this command is a miracle in and of itself. There was a bounty on Elijah's head, and King Ahab had searched all over the known world for him (1 Kings 18:10). Yet Elijah followed God's instruction to voluntarily present himself to the king who was trying to kill him.

But Elijah did not just settle for daring King Ahab; he was intent on daring the Eternal King!

When Ahab finally saw Elijah, his anger burned and he demanded, "Is that you, you troubler of Israel?" (v. 17).

Elijah's life was in danger, but King Ahab was desperate for an end to the drought. In a moment when any sane person would be focused on saving his own neck, Elijah aimed for much more. Rather than immediately delivering the news that the drought would soon end, he rebuked the king's sin: "'I have not made trouble for Israel,' Elijah replied. 'But you and your father's family have. You have abandoned the LORD's commands and have followed the Baals'" (v. 18). Elijah then ordered the king to summon the 450 prophets of Baal for a high-stakes challenge to determine the true God.

> Elijah dared the King to reveal Himself to the entire nation.

When all the people had gathered, Elijah addressed the crowd:

"How long will you waver between two opinions? If the LORD is God, follow him; but if Baal is God, follow him."

But the people said nothing.

Then Elijah said to them, "I am the only one of the LORD's prophets left, but Baal has four hundred and fifty prophets. Get two bulls for us. Let Baal's prophets choose one for themselves, and let them cut it into pieces and put it on the wood but not set fire to it. I will prepare the other bull and put it on the wood but not set fire to it. Then you call on the name of your god, and I will call on the name of the LORD. The god who answers by fire—he is God."

Then all the people said, "What you say is good." (vv. 21–24)

I am struck by the fact that God had not promised to deliver anything even similar to what Elijah was now publicly proclaiming. God had promised Elijah that He would send *rain*, not fire for an offering. Had Elijah simply been content to prophesy the coming rain, and that rain had indeed come, Elijah would have been received as a hero. But that was not enough for Elijah. He knew the power of his King, and he was determined to use this opportunity as a way for his King to demonstrate His power. He was not looking to save his own skin or even to convince King Ahab of the one true God. Elijah dared the King to reveal Himself to the entire nation.

The prophets of Baal went first. They prepared an altar

with a bull as a sacrifice and began to call on Baal to send down fire. They danced and called on Baal for several hours but received no answer. Halfway through the day, Elijah began to taunt the prophets: "Shout louder! Surely he is a god! Perhaps he is deep in thought, or busy, or traveling. Maybe he is sleeping and must be awakened" (v. 27). The prophets of Baal went so far as to cut themselves with swords and spears as they attempted to call down fire on their offering (v. 28).

But the idol god Baal was silent. The idol god Baal was idle. The idol god Baal did not have the power to deliver.

As Elijah stepped forward to take his turn in front of the people, he doubled and tripled down on his dare of the King:

Elijah took twelve stones, one for each of the tribes descended from Jacob, to whom the word of the LORD had come, saying, "Your name shall be Israel." With the stones he built an altar in the name of the LORD, and he dug a trench around it large enough to hold two seahs of seed. He arranged the wood, cut the bull into pieces and laid it on the wood. Then he said to them, "Fill four large jars with water and pour it on the offering and on the wood."

"Do it again," he said, and they did it again.

"Do it a third time," he ordered, and they did it

the third time. The water ran down around the altar and even filled the trench. (vv. 31–35)

Elijah was making it clear that there was no trickery or sleight of hand. He was creating the largest opening for a mighty act of the King that he possibly could. And he was tapping into a relationship with the King that is beyond anything I have ever experienced. Elijah had a relationship with the King that afforded him the ability to insist on His presence. How I desire the intimacy to confidently insist on the King's presence and power!

Once the stage was set, Elijah did not dance. He did not cut himself or even plead in a loud voice. He brashly set the stage for the King; then he humbled himself and simply asked the King to deliver:

LORD, the God of Abraham, Isaac and Israel, let it be known today that you are God in Israel and that I am your servant and have done all these things at your command. Answer me, LORD, answer me, so these people will know that you, LORD, are God, and that you are turning their hearts back again. (vv. 36–37)

To me, it feels as if Elijah was simply praying, "Come on, God; do this! I have done all I can to demonstrate that I don't hold the power. You do. It is time for You to show up!"

Then the fire of the LORD fell and burned up the sacrifice, the wood, the stones and the soil, and also licked up the water in the trench.

When all the people saw this, they fell prostrate and cried, "The LORD—he is God! The LORD—he is God!" (vv. 38–39)

The power of the King came down in an overwhelming fashion. As a result, the nation knelt before the King.

Elijah publicly dared the King to do the impossible. He was willing to *take crazy to the grave* if he had to, but he was unwilling to settle for anything less than the full power of the King. He was willing to set himself up to look ridiculous in order to give the King an opportunity to show His greatness. And he possessed an intimacy with the King that afforded him the confidence to insist on the King's delivery of that greatness: "Come on, God; do this!"

TAKE YOUR HOLY DARE

The time has come for you and me to issue our own Holy Dare. It is time for us to lay aside our weak faith and instead ask the King for great things. It is time for us to dare Him to use us in ways that are well outside our own strength. It is time for us to dare the King to show Himself mighty. It is time to call for His blessings to rain down, but let us not be satisfied with blessings alone. Let us press into an intimacy that affords us the courage to dare to ask for His mighty power to accompany those blessings. Is anything less really worth your life's service?

Ask yourself, "What is my holy dare? Do I have the courage to proclaim it?" With Elijah as our guide, we certainly have permission to proclaim and to insist on the King's power. He can handle the magnitude of our requests if we simply muster up the courage to set the grand stage and call Him to it.

Take the holy dare. Dare the King to be Who He claims to be. Put His name on the line, and place your name within His. That is the kind of courage and service that will bring nations to their knees.

WRESTLE WITH GOD

Much as we hesitate to dare the King, we act as if God cannot handle our honest questioning of Him. Our hesitation may be partially due to well-intentioned reverence, but I think it is mostly due to a plain, old-fashioned lack of courage. In a word, we are afraid to *wrestle*.

But if we are going to truly learn how to recognize the King's face, how to walk in a daily discovery of Him, and how to serve in His court, there will be times when we have to wrestle. We are going to have to wrestle with God, and we are going to have to wrestle with our flesh.

In Genesis 32, we are given an illustration of literal

wrestling with God in Jacob, the man who would become the father and the namesake of God's chosen people. The wrestling occurred as Jacob was attempting to obey the King's instruction and was the mechanism by which Jacob was blessed and his name changed to Israel.

To fully understand this pivotal moment, we must remember that Jacob had been living in a foreign land after fleeing the wrath of his brother, Esau. Jacob had stolen the birthright blessing that belonged to Esau, so he fled to a foreign land, where God blessed him with a large family and a huge amount of livestock. The last thing on Jacob's mind was returning to Esau—but the King had other plans.

Jacob's father-in-law became jealous of him. So the King commanded Jacob, "Go back to the land of your fathers and to your relatives, and I will be with you" (Genesis 31:3).

To obey this instruction, Jacob would have to leave everything he had worked for and return to a place where his life would be in danger. But Jacob obeyed and set off for home. Esau, upon hearing the news that his brother was returning, gathered four hundred men to go with him and meet Jacob. Jacob was so terrified of what his brother might do that he divided his family and his possessions into two separate camps, hoping that one camp would be able to escape if Esau attacked the other (Genesis 32:7–8).

It was in this state of mind that Jacob wrestled with God.

He had already been wrestling with God verbally over the command to return to Esau. His prayer that day included the desperate plea: "Save me, I pray, from the hand of my brother Esau" (v. 11). We can infer that Jacob did not receive sufficient assurance or comfort from God, because when night fell, Jacob sent both of his camps on ahead of him, but he stayed behind to continue his desperate conversation with God.

Instead of an evening of prayer, Jacob spent the night wrestling with God, who appeared in the form of a man to engage with Jacob. It is one

> How much do you want the blessing of the King?

of the most bizarre stories in a Bible full of bizarre stories. Genesis 32:22–32 tells of an all-night wrestling match that was so intense neither man could gain the upper hand. Upon realizing that Jacob would not relent, God—in the form of a man—reached out and dislocated Jacob's hip. But even in a disabled state, Jacob refused to let go. He insisted, "I will not let you go unless you bless me" (v. 26).

How much do you want the blessing of the King? Are you willing to serve Him in obedience even when commanded to do something that endangers your life? Are you willing to challenge Him to meet you in the place of that obedience in order to deliver you? Are you so desperate for His active participation in your life that you will lay aside timidity and challenge Him to reveal Himself and His ways to you? And when the confrontation with your King gets so intense that you are hobbled by it, will you be tenacious enough to demand His blessing upon you before you let go?

We have permission to wrestle with God with that kind of ferocity. In fact, it is what He desires of us. He longs for us to bring our doubts, our disbeliefs, and our challenges to Him in order for them to be tested. He wants to achieve intimacy with us, and He is hoping that we are desperate enough to insist on His blessing before we let go.

Of course, this God-man had sufficient power to cast Jacob aside. But He voluntarily brought Himself down to Jacob's level in order to gauge Jacob's level of desperation. Would Jacob hang on? Would he insist on a blessing?

Will you hang on? Will you dare to lay timidity aside and press into a wrestling match with the King? Will you insist on His blessing before letting go? True service to the King will require it. I assure you the King is ready to receive your challenge, and He is eager to bless you if you will just refuse to let go.

THE BENEFITS OF WRESTLING WITH GOD

There are two final takeaways from Jacob's wrestling match with God that we must not miss.

First, *wrestling with God gives us His identity*. When the God-man was finally convinced that Jacob was not going to let go, He blessed Jacob with these words: "Your name will no longer be Jacob, but Israel, because you have struggled with God and with humans and have overcome" (Genesis 32:28). The blessing of Jacob's struggle with God was a new identity. This identity not only promised an entire lineage that would have intimacy with the King but also means "he struggles with God."

Second, *wrestling with God allows us to see Him more clearly*. Please do not miss how Jacob (now Israel) described the result of his struggle with God. These pages are an effort to discover the face of the King through a service to Him. In Genesis 32:30, Jacob named the place where he wrestled with God Peniel, which means "face of God," and proclaimed, "It is because I saw God face to face, and yet my life was spared."

> We have permission to wrestle with God with that kind of ferocity.

If we truly want to know the face of the King, we might have to wrestle with Him. When a command to serve feels like more than you can bear, lay aside timidity and wrestle with the King. It is possible that the wrestling will leave you with a limp—as it did Jacob (v. 31), but you will leave having seen the face of God and with the assurance of His name stamped on your soul. Armed with that kind of assurance, you will find that the command you are called to carry out will seem like no challenge at all.

Dare the King. Wrestle with the King. He is willing and eager to meet your challenge.

CHAPTER FOURTEEN

Seek Justice

Learn to do right; seek justice.
Defend the oppressed.
Take up the cause of the fatherless;
plead the case of the widow.

Isaiah 1:17

J ustice is a central component of service to the King. It is a foundational plank in the platform of service we are building in order to proclaim the good news of the King. We are unequivocally instructed to pursue justice. But to do so, we must have a clear understanding of justice.

My professional career is devoted to seeking justice for the innocent and the oppressed. I am privileged to be associated with an organization that has made a definitional impact on what it means to *seek justice*. I have the unique opportunity to work for a leader with the clarity of vision to identify new ways to advocate for the oppressed and new methods of securing justice for the faithful. It is a blessing I cherish every day and an example I attempt to follow. After all, while obtaining justice is central to our discovery of the King, it is also extremely elusive.

Most times we think of justice in the prosecutorial sense. We think of the Department of Justice, the FBI, or the inside of a courtroom as a hardened criminal receives his just reward. I do not mean to suggest that these images are wrong, as the penalty for wrong actions certainly represents one side of the justice coin. It is the side that reminds us the penalty for our sin is death (Romans 6:23). There are consequences for wrong actions, and Scripture is replete with examples of people who are used to facilitate those consequences. But I have frequently confused my obligations for securing justice with the King's.

VENGEANCE IS THE KING'S

Romans 12:19 says, "Never take your own revenge, beloved, but leave room for the wrath of God, for it is written, 'VENGEANCE IS MINE, I WILL REPAY,' says the Lord" (NASB).

"Vengeance is Mine." When I see oppression in the world, vengeance is what my flesh instantly desires. When my work brings me to cases of innocent people who are being abused or persecuted, my first desire is to see the perpetrator punished. When I see entire groups of faithful people targeted for genocide, I want the crime to be avenged, and I want it avenged yesterday. In many ways, the desire is a holy one, as Romans 12:19 clearly tells us the King also wants vengeance for these types of wrongs.

> The vengeance piece of justice belongs to the King.

But we must never take ownership of that vengeance. The King owns the vengeance piece of justice, and it is a dangerous thing for us to forget. In fact, we see ever-increasing examples of the perversion of holy vengeance carried out in our world today. When people improperly assume the role of carrying out holy vengeance, the result is anything but holy. In fact, this unholy vengeance is taking the lives of the holy in many places around the world today. As we learn what it means to seek justice, we must first understand how to lay down our desire for vengeance. The vengeance piece of justice belongs to the King.

DEFEND THE OPPRESSED

Our role in seeking justice lies on the side of defending the oppressed.

The wake of injustice leaves a trail of victims who are in need of restoration. It is this trail of victims that represents our portion of the holy charge to obtain justice. Vengeance belongs to the King; *our command is to run to the oppressed.* Our instruction is to intervene on behalf of the victim. Our holy charge is to restore those who have been widowed and orphaned (both literally and figuratively) by injustice. We do not need a "calling" or a directive to engage in this pursuit of justice, because we have already been called—even commanded—to do it.

Micah 6:8 reminds us to quit wondering what we have been called to, because we have already been told what we are called to:

He has shown you, O mortal, what is good.
And what does the LORD require of you?

To act justly and to love mercy
  and to walk humbly with your God.

We are called to a humble walk with the King that embodies love and justice. The command to "walk humbly with
your God" is mostly reflective of our vertical relationship with
Him. But the commands to "act justly" and to "love mercy"
are mostly reflective of our horizontal responsibilities to the
world around us. They are commands to learn how to pursue
a grace-filled justice that rescues the oppressed. It is not a
one-time thing, or even a once-in-a-while endeavor. Rather,
we are called to live in perpetual service to the oppressed.

There will be times when we are called to "bring justice"
to wrongdoers, but vengeance is the King's and the King's
alone. Our duty is to the oppressed.

THE QUEEN'S PEOPLE

The story of Esther is a beautiful illustration of our duty to
seek justice for those around us. In so many ways, it is a
story of tremendous scandal and intrigue. It is a made-for-
TV script with heroes and villains, and plenty of uncertainty
about which characters fall into which category. But in the
end, it is a story that demonstrates the importance of yielding
to the King's plans, as they are so much higher than those we
have crafted based on the circumstances we can see.

We often begin Esther's story near the end of Esther 2,

when a crown was placed upon her head and she was made queen. But Esther 1 gives us the uncomfortable backdrop. King Xerxes was terribly drunk and out of control as a result of an extravagant, weeklong party. On the seventh day of this raging party, Xerxes decided it would be a good idea to summon his wife, Queen Vashti, to the party so the revelers could gawk at her. King Xerxes's command was not veiled:

> On the seventh day, when King Xerxes was in high spirits from wine, he commanded the seven eunuchs who served him . . . to bring before him Queen Vashti, wearing her royal crown, in order to display her beauty to the people and nobles, for she was lovely to look at. (Esther 1:10–11)

The king wanted his drunk friends to leer at his wife. Queen Vashti did what any respectable woman would do in the face of such a ridiculous request—she refused. Because Queen Vashti refused to be objectified by drunken partiers, King Xerxes took away her crown and banished her from his presence (vv. 15–22). In short, Esther 1 paints the picture of an angry, alcoholic king with a penchant for objectifying women. King Xerxes was the kind of man every woman wants to avoid. Then it got worse.

King Xerxes ordered a nationwide search for beautiful women in order to form a personal harem (Esther 2:1–4).

The petulant, chauvinist, angry, alcoholic king was forming a harem, and it was for this reason that Esther caught his eye. Too often, we skip past the horrific circumstances of this story. We read the Cinderella-style fairy tale of a common girl becoming queen rather than the harsh reality of a girl taken from her home and placed in a harem for a volatile, dangerous drunkard. I am fairly confident that Esther hoped the king would choose a different girl.

But the king chose Esther, and Esther became the queen (v. 17).

Esther was not looking for an injustice to correct. Esther was *the victim of an injustice.*

JUSTICE AGAINST THE ODDS

King Xerxes was not the only villain in Esther's story. Haman, one of the king's nobles, had convinced the king that everyone should kneel before Haman when he passed. But Mordecai, a Jew (and Esther's cousin, unbeknownst to Haman), refused to kneel before Haman. In a shocking display of the volatility of both men, Haman convinced the king to order the execution of all the Jews in the land (Esther 3). The fact that Haman convinced the king to issue this order is even more remarkable given that Mordecai had proven his loyalty to the king by uncovering and foiling a plot to assassinate the king (Esther 2:19–23). But the king—in yet another demonstration that he was a violent, arrogant, power-hungry ruler—cast aside the good that Mordecai had shown him and ordered the annihilation of the Jews.

Meanwhile, Esther had understandably been focused on her own complicated situation. She was not looking for, nor did she have the capacity to take on, the plight of an entire people slated for destruction. But these were not just any people. They were *her* people. And Esther was no longer just a girl. Esther was the *queen*. God had used an extraordinarily bad set of circumstances to move Esther to a place where He could use her to bring about justice. He had not required her to search out an injustice to address but had brought that injustice to her.

> Esther was not looking for an injustice to correct. Esther was *the victim of an injustice.*

Too often we act as if we cannot address the injustices that surround us. We act as if they are someone else's problem or as if we are powerless to address them. Esther was just a girl forced into the harem of an angry, drunken king. Her position of authority existed only because her predecessor had responsibly refused to cater to the perverted whims of the king Esther was now serving. Esther's options were few, and she was anything but untouchable. In fact, she was as vulnerable as it is possible to be, and she knew it. Yet it was in that vulnerable state that Esther was called upon to save her people from annihilation. It was on that precarious footing that Esther's stand for the oppressed would occur.

So, "Where, and for whom, am I called to pursue justice?" you ask. If Esther is any example, we do not have to go searching for the opportunity. The desperate needs of the oppressed will find us—*and we might even be among the oppressed.* The question is whether we accept that pursuit of justice on behalf of the oppressed.

Even with the fate of all her people hanging in the balance, Esther was conflicted about whether she should intervene, and if so, how to intervene. The destruction of the Jews was imminent, but if Esther approached the king uninvited, it was very likely she would be killed. The girl who had been forced into the harem of a violent drunk—and who was now clinging to a position of power that was only hers because her predecessor dared to cross the king—was now being asked to cross the king. She was being asked to violate the order to approach the king only when summoned, and she was being asked to do so for the purpose of confronting the king about another of his orders. She knew the king was likely to respond as most violent drunks would—and as the king had done in the past: vengefully. Esther's situation was extremely dire, to say the least. But Mordecai reminded

> Each of us is charged with the pursuit of justice for the afflicted.

Esther that she would not escape the coming wrath, and then he implored her, "Who knows but that you have come to your royal position for such a time as this?" (Esther 4:14).

Each of us is charged with the pursuit of justice for the afflicted. Each of us has certain positions of influence—be they large or small—that we may be called to leverage for that pursuit. Let us be mindful of Mordecai's reminder that our positions of influence do not exist simply for their own sake, but rather specifically for such a time as this, when justice must be pursued.

We live in days marked by injustice, but we have a position of royalty. We are part of a royal priesthood that serves the King. We are very likely the conduits through which justice for the oppressed must flow.

Who are the oppressed around you?

What position of influence do you hold that might alter the reality of those oppressed?

What are the causes that surround you that may in fact be the very reasons for your call to this time and place?

Will you dare to approach the King unannounced on behalf of the oppressed around you?

Esther responded this way:

> Go, gather together all the Jews who are in Susa, and fast for me. Do not eat or drink for three days, night or day. I and my attendants will fast as you do. When

this is done, I will go to the king, even though it is against the law. And if I perish, I perish. (v. 16)

The circumstances had not changed. Esther still believed she would likely die at the hands of the king. But she also knew that she had been called to this time and place in order to pursue justice for the oppressed, so she pressed in.

Do we value our call to the oppressed above our own lives? I confess to you that I cannot claim to have achieved this focus. But it is what the King calls us to. It is what service to the King looks like. If we desire to serve Him, and if we desire to channel His power, it requires the laying down of our lives.

TRUTH TO POWER

Once we commit to pursuing justice for the oppressed, we must contemplate the best way to speak truth to the earthly powers who can deliver it. I mentioned earlier that I am grateful to be associated with an organization that finds creative ways to engage earthly authorities and achieve results that should not have been possible. Esther did precisely that, and her three days of fasting and prayer must have delivered the shrewd plan that she carried out.

When Esther approached the king, not only did he extend his scepter and receive Esther, but he made her this stunning offer: "What is it, Queen Esther? What is your request? Even up to half the kingdom, it will be given you" (Esther 5:3).

If ever there was an opportunity to make a request on behalf of a people slated for annihilation, it is when you have just been offered up to half of the king's kingdom! But Esther wisely understood that her request was even more significant than half of the kingdom, so she responded, "If it pleases the king, let the king, together with Haman, come today to a banquet I have prepared for him" (v. 4). The king loved banquets, so he readily agreed. As the banquet came to a close, the king again asked Esther what she wanted, but again Esther refrained and simply invited the king and Haman to another feast the next day, where she promised to reveal her petition.

I am struck by this often-overlooked portion of the story. As Esther was pursuing a king for the cause of justice, *the* King was preparing a way for that justice to be delivered. As Haman returned home that evening—likely in a rather drunken state—he saw Mordecai in the king's court and was filled with hatred for him. After consulting his wife and friends—and boasting about his great favor with both the king and queen—Haman ordered a fifty-cubit pole to be erected and schemed to make a request of the king in the morning that Mordecai be impaled on the pole.

The stakes were set. Haman and Esther had diametrically opposite requests for the king, and the almighty King had made provision for the very thing that was intended for evil to be used to accomplish His justice. The vessel for carrying out that justice was Queen Esther—the girl who was forced into the harem of a violent, drunk king, and who faced annihilation at the hands of the king's closest adviser.

As the king struggled to sleep—no doubt dealing with holy heartburn as a result of Queen Esther's banquet—he ordered his servants to read to him from the official records and was reminded of the occasion when Mordecai saved the king's life. The king was moved to honor Mordecai immediately and looked around for someone to help him do so. It was at this moment that Haman entered the courtyard. The king summoned Haman and asked for his advice on how to honor a man who had pleased the king. Haman, thinking he was that man, suggested a series of very public actions that he wanted to have bestowed on himself. The king agreed with Haman's proposal and ordered Haman to personally facilitate the honors . . . upon Mordecai!

Queen Esther's petition for justice had not even been submitted, and already *the* King is using her obedience to redeem what was intended for evil for good. But it was only a precursor to the second day of banqueting and Esther's ultimate request for mercy.

When the king again asked Esther what she wanted and promised her up to half his kingdom, Esther finally revealed that she and her people were about to be destroyed and begged the king for mercy. The king's famous rage now boiled over and he demanded to know who was behind the plot. Esther responded, "An adversary and enemy! This vile Haman!" (Esther 7:6). The king's rage grew further, and as Haman begged Esther for his life, the king decided Haman's fate and ordered him impaled on the very pole he had erected for Mordecai's execution (vv. 9–10).

The King had called the girl forced into the harem of a violent, drunk king to a pursuit of justice for the oppressed. That girl's obedience paved the way for not only the salvation of an oppressed people but also a magnificent display of power from *the* King. In the aftermath of Haman's execution, the king issued a new edict allowing the Jews to defend themselves and Mordecai was elevated to Haman's position of power and authority (Esther 8:1–17).

However, the real lesson is found in Esther's pursuit of justice. There were countless reasons for Esther to focus on her unfortunate past and her catastrophic circumstances. But instead she focused on the question "Where, and for whom, am I called to pursue justice?" She recognized that she had been called to her position of royalty "for such a time as this," and she boldly spoke truth to the earthly powers through whom justice could flow.

Our service to the King is incomplete if our commitment to justice for the oppressed is anything less. I challenge you to join me in considering these questions:

"Who are the oppressed around me?"

"What leverage might I have to seek justice on their behalf?"

"How can I speak truth to power for those without a voice?"

There is certainly risk to seeking justice on behalf of the oppressed and downtrodden. But even so we must not lay down the duty to constantly be in search of justice for the oppressed. If we perish, we perish. But our obedience may be the very thing that saves an entire people. And our service to the King is incomplete if it does not answer the charge to *do justly*.

CHAPTER FIFTEEN

Be the One

*The LORD looks down from heaven
on all mankind to see if there are any who understand,
any who seek God. All have turned away,
all have become corrupt;
there is no one who does good, not even one.*

Psalm 14:2–3

I want to change this generation. I look around and I see so much separation from the King. I see my generation and the ones after it chasing things that are not only inconsistent with the King's mission but also directly hostile to it. I see a lack of passion for the King's Word and an absence of discipline for knowing His ways. Maybe the most troubling of all is that I see that same reflection in my own soul. There is an unmistakable pull toward things that bear no semblance of royalty—things that I know good and well will burn and pass away one day (2 Peter 3:10). And yet my longing for them remains. I see all of this, and it leads me to ask this question: "How do I change the generation?"

How do I change the generation (myself included) in favor of service to the King? It seems like a daunting challenge. No, that is selling it short. It feels insurmountable. It seems like an impossible task. It seems impossible because it *is* impossible (at least in the way I am asking the question). Each of us has a heart that is "desperately wicked" (Jeremiah 17:9 KJV) and inclined to things that take us away from the King. If our focus is first on changing the generation, then we will fail.

Fortunately, it is not up to me to turn the hearts of the generation. Psalm 14 says the King is looking down on all mankind for any who love and seek Him, and He finds "no one . . . not even one" (v. 3). At first, I am even more depressed upon hearing this news. It feels like a stamp of permanency on the lost state of my generation. There is not even *one*, God? How can that be?

It is with grief—but followed quickly by hope—that I realize the "no one . . . not even one" declaration includes me. *It includes me.* As the King has been going to and fro to the ends of the earth (2 Chronicles 16:9), He is searching for just one who is faithful. This should not surprise me, as it is precisely what He did in Genesis 6 before destroying the earth with the Flood. He searched for, and found, only one who was upright. Genesis 6:8 says, "Noah found favor in the eyes of the LORD." Noah was the one. He was the one who pursued the King even while the generation around him abandoned the King. And because Noah was the one, he and those he loved were spared.

The King is holy and jealous, and there is a price to pay for choosing to reject Him. But He is also abundantly patient and forgiving. He is desperate to find just one who is faithful. He is searching to the ends of the earth to find the one who is desperate for Him. He is not looking for those worthy of His wrath. No, He is searching for the one. He is searching for the one He can save. Just *one*.

Here is the great hope in this reality: I do not have to change this generation. I just have to change me. I just have to *be the one*.

Now, it is a good thing for our hearts to be tugged toward our generation and their salvation. In fact, we are commanded to take the good news into all the world (Mark 16:15), because the King desires that none should perish (2 Peter 3:9). But notice how God's mercy was realized through Noah. It was realized as the result of *one* man focusing on *one* thing: being the *one*. Noah made sure that when the King looked down to see if there were any who seek God, he would be found. He would be faithful. He would *be the one*. As a result, more than just a generation was saved. As a result of Noah being the one, all of mankind was given another chance.

> I do not have to change the generation. I just have to change me. I just have to *be the one*.

If we want to change the generation, it starts in our own hearts and in our own lives.

The King is now going to and fro looking for one who is faithful. When His eyes sweep over you, be ready. Be found in the King. *Be the one*.

SEARCH, DISCOVER, SERVE

In these pages, we have discussed three phases of intimacy with the King: searching for the King, discovering the King, and serving the King. It is less important which phase you currently find yourself in and more important which direction you are heading. Are you growing in intimacy with the King or are you regressing? Or maybe you have become content where you are?

The enemy is desperate to convince us that complacency is acceptable. He is working tirelessly to rob us of the joy and fulfillment that come from a life infused with the King's presence and power. His first goal is to take us out of relationship with the King, but upon failing to accomplish that, he is eager to inject us with complacency and stall our relationship with the King wherever it is along this spectrum. This is the "steal" portion of the enemy's goal to "steal and kill and destroy" our intimacy with the King (John 10:10).

It is worth noting that just as the King walks to and fro looking for one who is faithful, the enemy "prowls around like a roaring lion looking for someone to devour" (1 Peter 5:8). It is a bit of a cosmic game of hide-and-seek, with the Lion of Judah seeking one who is faithful and the enemy prowling like a lion seeking to destroy that one.

I will note, however, that there is only one true lion in this analogy. The enemy is *posing* as a lion. He is an imposter. He is prowling around *like a lion* in an attempt to interrupt our intimacy with the King. This is yet another reason that it is vital for us to be able to identify the King. We have to know the King's face. We must be desperate to identify the King and to be found in Him.

So how can we be assured we are found in—and by—the King while remaining hidden and protected from the imposter? The answer lies in the pursuit of discovery and service we have been discussing in these pages. It lies in the assurance that we are moving in the proper direction along this knowing/discovering/serving spectrum. Our pursuit of intimacy with the King has a starting point (the moment we yield to Him by believing in our hearts and confessing with our mouths that He is Lord), but it does not have a finish line on this side of heaven. Until that day when He comes in glory and all is revealed to us, we will find ourselves at varying stages of this process. In one area, we will walk in greater discovery and service to the King than we might in another. But the key is our focus and our direction. Are we moving toward discovery and service? That is what will allow us to be shielded from the imposter and found by the King.

WALK IN OBEDIENCE

When the King found Noah alone to be faithful among all the earth, it was because Noah had searched out an intimate knowledge of the King. He is described as "a righteous man, blameless among the people of his time, and he walked faithfully with God" (Genesis 6:9). Noah was a righteous man, and because of it he was saved, along with his family.

But Noah was in the first of our three stages. He had searched for the King and possessed a thorough knowledge of the King. He had faithfully learned who the King was and carefully followed the King's commands. Noah was righteous because he was pursuing the King and had acquired an intimate understanding of the King's identity. Noah knew the King's name and the King's ways.

But Noah was about to step into the second stage: discovery of the King. His faithfulness in knowing the King had saved him to this point. But in order for that salvation to last, Noah was going to have to walk in obedience as he was called into a deeper discovery of the King. If at any point Noah had chosen complacency and decided to rest in the simple knowledge of the King—a knowledge that had served him so well to this point—he would have been lost.

When Noah was growing from knowledge to discovery and receiving detailed instructions for building the ark, a failure to walk in that discovery would have spelled disaster. Discovery of the King takes us beyond the attributes of the King and into receipt of His instructions. Discovery moves us into position to take action. Discovery is the transition from understanding to action. It is the moment when the King is enabled to give us a charge for our generation.

Then, as Noah moved into the third stage, from discovery to service, a failure to walk in service would have proven equally devastating. Had Noah been content to have discovered and conversed with the King, but had failed to put the King's plan into action, he would have perished. Had Noah chosen to boast about his receipt of the King's plans rather than taking up the backbreaking service that was building the ark, it would have all been for naught.

Service to the King takes us beyond receipt of His instructions and into implementation of them. Service to the King is the moment of action. It is the realization of ownership in the King's mission. It is the conversion from *being charged* to *charging forward*. And yes, it is the backbreaking work of felling trees, hand-planing those trees into planks, and driving them nail by nail and board by board into an enormous floating box that will protect us from some threat we have never heard of. Service means enduring the mocking of people in order to receive the adulation of the King. It means taking on a bit of crazy and daring the King to show up and show off His power. Service to the King means laying down our ways and taking up His.

Service is hard. It is sometimes arduous. But it is the only way to truly satisfy our search for the king. And it is the only way to really discover the King.

COMMITTED TO SERVICE

When Noah was given instructions to build a giant floating box to protect himself from a threat he had never heard of, he was five hundred years old. He was far too old to take on this task, never mind the animal care that would follow. But Noah's call to service was clear: decades of grueling labor, followed by a year of animal care in a giant floating box. There is no doubt that in the eyes of those who were watching Noah, a decision to move from discovery to service of the King would convert him from an old man into a *crazy* old man. Logic said to refuse the instruction. Common sense said to choose sanity over insanity. Intellect demanded that Noah take a more responsible path.

But Noah knew the King was walking to and fro, looking for just *one*. Noah knew the imposter was also prowling like a lion, seeking to steal his intimacy with the King, kill him and his family, and destroy the King's plans. Noah chose to turn in to the insanity. Noah pursued the King. Noah ran toward discovery. Noah committed to service. And in doing so, Noah's pursuit of the King became a discovery of the King, and that discovery became a service to the King.

That service to the King saved a generation and all of the generations that followed. That service to the King saved you, and it saved me.

Do you desire to change this generation? The requirement is simple: *serve the King.*

BEGIN TODAY

Where do you find yourself in this search for the king? Have you reached a point of acknowledging that not just any king will do, and that to truly resolve your search, you will need an encounter with *the* King? If so, the King is waiting with open arms and is eager to begin a relationship with you. Romans 10:9 confirms that the requirements for acceptance by the King are extraordinarily simple: you must simply tell Him of your belief that He is Lord and that God raised Him from the dead. That is it. If you are taking that step today, welcome to an eternity with the King! I encourage you to seek out others who will share in the rest of this discovery with you.

> Where do you find yourself in this search for the king?

Maybe you find yourself in a place where you know the King and have been saved by His grace, but you are not experiencing a daily, dynamic, interactive dialogue with the King. You know and love the King, but you want to know more of Him. You desire intimacy and tangible evidence of your relationship with Him. In short, you want a fresh discovery of the King. If that is you, I challenge you to be like Shasta and muster the courage to whisper the question: "Who are you?" Invite the King to speak to you about His identity. Surrender your desires in favor of freely kneeling to His will. Invite the King to fill you with His power. Make a decision that you will settle for nothing less than the full power and authority of the King in your daily life.

Finally, maybe you know the King and have walked in His power. Maybe you know intimacy with Him but long to know it even more. Perhaps you know what it means to serve the King but desire to achieve a new level of commitment to that service. I challenge you to respond to that longing today. Ask the King—yes, even *dare* the King—to show up in your life and show off His power through you. Posture your life in a way that prioritizes service to others, but do it in a fashion that insists on the King's presence and power. Step onto the grand stage without fear. Proclaim the name of the King and your association within His name. Stake your reputation on the King's and set the scene for Him to come through. Then buckle in and brace yourself, because you are about to experience His mighty power at work in and through you!

In so many ways, our world is on fire. But we have no reason to fear, because we serve the King. You desire to change the world, and in the King's might, you can do just that. But the way to change the world is through a life committed to discovering the King and dedicated to service in His court. The way to make an impact that will echo beyond your years is to simply be found continually in Him.

Begin today. Be found in the King. *Be the one.*

Acknowledgments

When I write, my words are but mere echoes of those who have spoken truth and light into my life. They are echoes of the King because so many have lent their voices to the King by way of investment in me. The message of this book, and any ability I have to deliver it, is because of those faithful voices. They are far too numerous to name exhaustively, but I am deeply grateful to each one. These are but a few of those voices.

To my bride, Brooke, the love of my life. Thank you for being my partner in our ongoing discovery of the King. Thank you for your patience with me when that discovery is elusive. Thank you for speaking life into this project, even before there was evidence of life in it. I cannot wait to continue discovering with you.

To my children, Jude, Brell, and Hope. You guys make life fun! I love you infinitely more than the breath in my lungs. There is nobody I would rather be than your dad.

To my blood dad and mom, Steve and Melody. Thank you for pointing me toward the King and encouraging me to run to Him. You are the foundational reason I am in love with Jesus.

To my chosen dad and mom, Jim and Jan. You cover me—and have covered this project—in prayer like none other, and I am deeply grateful. Thank you for grafting me as your own.

To my blood siblings, Heather, Heidi, Matthew, Isaac, Holly, and Stevan Jr. Thank you for showing me so many expressions of Jesus and for believing in my ability to speak this message despite an intimate knowledge of my shortcomings.

To my chosen siblings, Chris, Kipp, Jenna, Blake, and Isaac. Thank you for choosing to be a part of this wild and crazy Bennett name and for injecting fresh dreams into all of us. Our family would be incomplete without you.

To my pastor, Mark Batterson. Your weekly words over the last fifteen years are no doubt reflected in this book. Thank you for faithfully speaking into this project for so many years, and for so long before I finally took it on. Thank you for getting me out of the starting blocks on April 19, 2015, and for lending your voice to the foreword. Your belief in this project and in me played a major role in bringing it to reality.

To my agent, Shannon Marven. Your belief in my writing was a true turning point in this process. You caught the vision of my heart in a way that made me desperate to be on your team. Your tireless work dramatically exceeded every cost-benefit analysis. I am deeply honored to call you my friend and teammate in this endeavor. Your entire team at Dupree Miller—and a special nod to Nicki Miser for her attention to detail for me—is second to none!

To everyone at Worthy Publishing—Byron Williamson, Jeana Ledbetter, Leeanna Nelson, Nicole Pavlas, Caroline Green, and the rest of the team who put so much effort into making this project a reality. Thank you for seeing the vision for this book when it was only a verbally delivered mustard seed! Thank you for your refining input at every stage—conceptual, organizational, and editorial. I am humbled to have the privilege of working with such a great team.

To my editor, Jennifer Stair. I am indebted to you for your incredible investment of time, energy, expertise, and passion to make sure this message is delivered in a way that will impact readers toward the King. This project is immeasurably better because of your trained eye, skilled hand, and caring heart.

To two of my mentors, Jay and Pam Sekulow. For more

than a decade now I have had a front-row seat as you have modeled what dedicated service to the King looks like. I am intensely grateful for your example to me, for your investment in me, and for your belief in this endeavor.

To my aunt, Eileen Hooley. Thank you for being my first reader. Your feedback was both encouraging and constructive, but it was your heart for the King that spurred me on the most.

To my friend Nicole Smith. Thank you for your generosity and skilled contributions to the digital support for this project. You can attest that I desperately needed your guidance!

To my brother Isaac and my friend Bob Powers. The two of you faithfully pushed me to start writing for many years, even as I continued to resist. By the grace of God and thanks in no small part to your loving but firm prodding, I have written.

To the countless others who have contributed support and encouragement to this project. I am deeply grateful and openly acknowledge that this book is only a reality because of all of you. While I can never fully repay your kindness, I have faith that your efforts will have an impact for the King that echoes into eternity.

Notes

Introduction: Where Is the King?

1. C. S. Lewis, *The Horse and His Boy*, The Chronicles of Narnia (New York: HarperCollins, 1994).
2. Ibid., 174.
3. Ibid.
4. See Acts 2:2; Genesis 2:7; and Job 33:4 for just a few examples.
5. Lewis, *The Horse and His Boy*, 175–76.

Chapter 1: Who Is the King?

1. Helen H. Lemmel, "Turn Your Eyes Upon Jesus," 1922.

Chapter 2: The King's Credentials

1. There are numerous prophecies about Jesus's arrival that, combined with the story of His birth, illustrate the significance of His humble beginnings. If you would like to study this further, I recommend reading Micah 5:2 against the backdrop of the Gospels' depiction of Jesus's birth. In summary, Jesus arrived in a humble fashion and from pedestrian lineage in order to fully demonstrate that His kingdom is not rooted in temporal authority.
2. There are numerous Old Testament prophecies on this point, as well as New Testament realizations of these prophecies. For a deeper study on this topic, I recommend starting with the numerous prophecies in Isaiah 53, and the accompanying fulfillments in Matthew 20:28; Ephesians 5:2; Galatians 1:4; 1 John 2:2; Hebrews 9:28; and 2 Corinthians 5:21.

Chapter 3: The Eternal King

1. Revelation 3:4–5; 6:11; 7:9–13; and 19:14 are just a few examples.

Chapter 5: The King Who Walks with Us

1. Genesis 4 and Jude v. 14 refer to a different Enoch.

Chapter 6: Discovery over Pursuit

1. Paul Scalia, "Funeral Homily for Justice Antonin Scalia," *First Things*, February 22, 2016, https://www.firstthings.com/web-exclusives/2016/02/funeral-homily-for -justice-antonin-scalia.

Chapter 8: Echoes

1. Thank you to Aoife Torpey with Ireland's Office of Public Works for providing the precise wording.

Chapter 10: Surrender

1. Matthew 26:39–42; Mark 14:36; and Luke 22:42.
2. A brief description of Pierce's inspiration to write these words may be found at https://www.samaritanspurse.org/our-ministry/history.
3. Romans 14:11; Philippians 2:10; and Isaiah 45:23.

Chapter 11: Choose Service

1. Matthew 20:28; Mark 10:45; 1 Timothy 2:6; and Hebrews 9:15.
2. See also Mark 9:35 and Matthew 23:11.
3. Romans 12:5 and 1 Corinthians 12:20, among many other examples.

About the Author

THANN BENNETT and his wife, Brooke, live in Fort Washington, Maryland, with their three children: Jude, Gambrell, and Hope. The Bennetts are longtime members of the National Community Church family in Washington, D.C. In his professional capacity, Thann is the Director of Government Affairs for the American Center for Law and Justice. He has sixteen years of high-level public policy experience, with a particular focus on the US Congress and the United Nations. He is also a regular on-air contributor to the daily syndicated radio broadcast, *Jay Sekulow Live!* Thann originally hails from the cornfields of Central Illinois and is a lifelong Chicago Cubs fan. He is motivated to write by a belief that God calls those in all walks of life to draw others to a saving knowledge of Jesus Christ.

IF YOU ENJOYED THIS BOOK, WILL YOU CONSIDER SHARING THE MESSAGE WITH OTHERS?

Mention the book in a blog post or through Facebook, Twitter, Pinterest, or upload a picture through Instagram.

Recommend this book to those in your small group, book club, workplace, and classes.

Head over to facebook.com/worthypublishing, "LIKE" the page, and post a comment as to what you enjoyed the most.

Tweet "I recommend reading #InSearchOfTheKing by @ThannBennett // @worthypub"

Pick up a copy for someone you know who would be challenged and encouraged by this message.

Write a book review online.

Visit us at worthypublishing.com

twitter.com/worthypub

worthypub.tumblr.com

facebook.com/worthypublishing

pinterest.com/worthypub

instagram.com/worthypub

youtube.com/worthypublishing